11+ MATHS PRACTICE PAPERS

Thorough Answers & In-Depth Guided Explanations

ANTHONY RAJECKI-DOYLE

Copyright © 2022 Accolade Tuition Ltd
Published by Accolade Tuition Ltd
71-75 Shelton Street
Covent Garden
London WC2H 9JQ
www.accoladetuition.com
info@accoladetuition.com

ISBN 978-1-913988-28-9

FIRST EDITION
1 3 5 7 9 10 8 6 4 2

Contents

Exam Paper Eight

Foreword

The 11+ mathematics papers administered by top schools (be they independent powerhouses, or high-flying grammars) can be deeply challenging. Not only do they frequently present students with problems in unfamiliar contexts, but they also require candidates to answer a large number of questions under heavy time pressure.

Indeed, 11+ maths papers typically consist of dozens of questions, each of which a student might only be able to spend a couple of minutes on in order to keep pace. This is why it is essential for students not simply to have a basic understanding of the topics they have covered thus far in school (be it arithmetic, geometry, or algebra), but to have an advanced familiarity that allows them to rapidly identify the crux of a problem and then tackle it swiftly. This must be done a number of times, in quick succession, across a range of topics.

For the vast majority of pupils, this level of familiarity can only be achieved through exposure to the same core ideas in many different contexts — in other words, *practice, practice and practice*! But while this may seem daunting, there is a distinct upside: it means that achieving the highest grades is within reach for any dedicated student with enough self-belief and the right work ethic!

As you work though this volume, you will encounter problems that will stump even the brightest mathematicians — questions that may leave you wondering where to start. More often than not, what will be tripping you up will not be a lack of understanding: it will be the challenge of applying concepts you've learned in class in new and unusual contexts. This book will serve as a roadmap that not only sketches out answers to tricky questions, but also explains, in detail, how to navigate such unorthodox problems, while arming you with tips and tricks that will allow you to tackle any challenge an 11+ paper might throw your way.

Rest assured that working through the papers in this volume will give you ample opportunity to grapple with the topics you are likely to be grilled on. And it will also allow you get comfortable with the time pressures involved with the 11+ exams, and to build the stamina you'll need to prevail!

How This Book Is Set Out

After an extensive review of materials from dozens of the most competitive schools in the country, we have developed eight entirely novel exam papers. These papers, as you would expect, reflect the difficulty of the papers issued by these schools, while also covering the diverse range of topics on which candidates are expected to be deeply well versed.

Care has been taken to include problems that require innovative thinking — or that put a unique spin on classroom materials. These trickier questions, however, tend to appear near the end of each paper. In the earlier portions of each paper, candidates will find instead a good number of more straightforward "warm-up" questions. Yet while these are less challenging, it is important that they are also taken seriously. Plenty of students drop easy marks on them as a result of clumsy mistakes or a lack of familiarity. The more you are drilled on the fundamentals, and the more swiftly you can tackle these earlier questions, the more time you have to work through the more challenging latter half of the paper.

The questions for each paper appear twice. The first time they appear by themselves, so that students can, if they wish, have a go at tackling the paper. They will then appear a second time, but this time accompanied by answers and detailed guidance.

Each paper will include a "time guide" – that is, the amount of time one would expect to be given to complete the paper in an exam hall.

You will notice that you are not told how many marks any given question in these papers is worth. In short, while some schools *do* specify how many marks questions are worth, most others do not. In our view, *not* being told is far more challenging – after all, it requires the student to use their intuition to gauge how many marks a question is likely to be worth based on its difficulty, and thus how much time they ought to dedicate to each question.

Since our intention with this guide is to prepare students for the very trickiest papers they are likely to encounter, we decided to adopt this more common (and more difficult!) format. Don't be discouraged if it takes you a little while to develop a radar for how to allocate your time: you will get the hang of it as you work through the volume.

There is no *correct* way to use this guide. Some students will feel comfortable working through it by themselves, whereas some may prefer to have a parent at hand to act as a kind of surrogate tutor. In any case, the intention of this book is to give the student the experience of having an experienced tutor at their beck and call.

Best of luck as you work through this paper. And remember: *practice, practice, practice*!

Anthony Rajecki-Doyle, October 2022

Exam Paper One

60 Minutes | 20 Questions

Practice Paper One
60 MINUTES: 20 QUESTIONS

1. Work out: 350 + 121 + 52

Answer:_____

2. Work out: 34 x 56

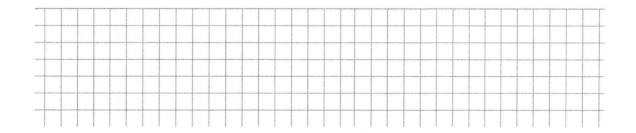

Answer:_____

3. Work out: 20.1 ÷ 3

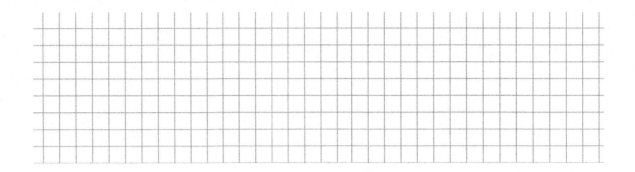

Answer:_____

4. Work out: -1 - 5.1

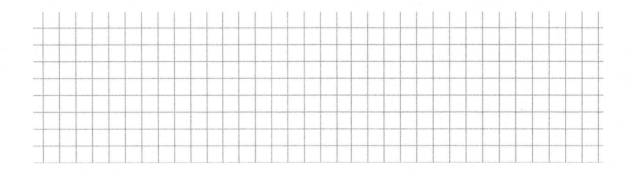

Answer:_____

5. What are the missing terms in each of the following sequences:

    a) 4, 10, ___, 22, 28, ___

    b) ___, ___, 22, 18, 14

    c) 1024, 512, 256, 128, ___, ___

    d) 7, 4, 1, ___, ___

    e) 1, 4, 9, 16, ___, ___

6. Which of the numbers below are multiples of 74:

74	1	148
37	7474	370

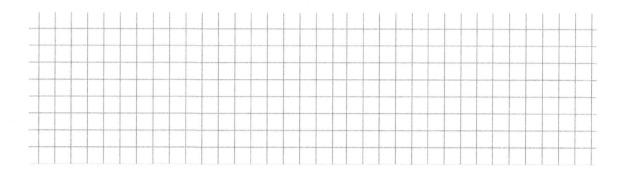

Answer:_____

7. A train is travelling from Bristol to Norwich. The train leaves at 13:43pm and arrives at 00:13am.

a. How long is this journey in hours and minutes?

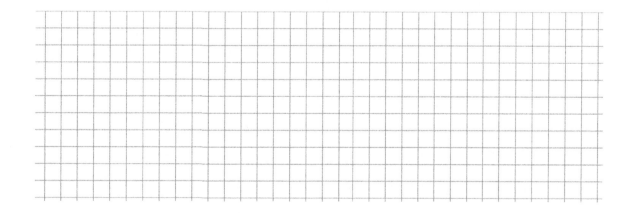

Answer:_____

b. The distance from Bristol to Norwich is 210 miles. What is the speed of the train in mph?

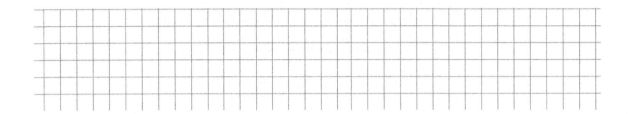

Answer:_____

8. a. What is the mean, median and mode of the following list of numbers:

8, 45, 6, 3, 1, 6, 3, 3, 15

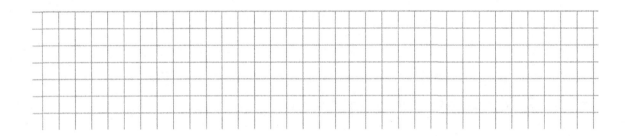

Mean:_____   Median:_____   Mode:_____

b. Two other numbers are added to this list and the mean does not change. One is 19, what is the other number?

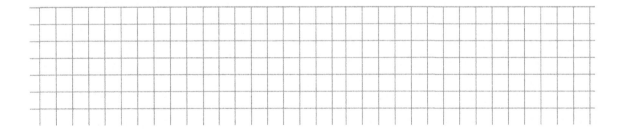

Answer:_____

9. Below you can see angles labelled on a triangle.

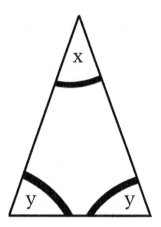

    a. If x = 40, find y.

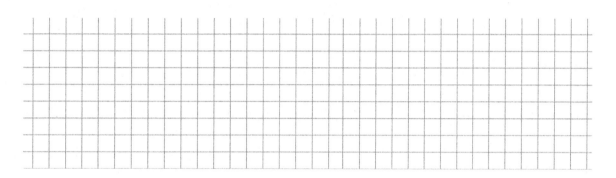

                                               Answer:_____

b. If x = 60, how many lines of symmetry does the triangle have?

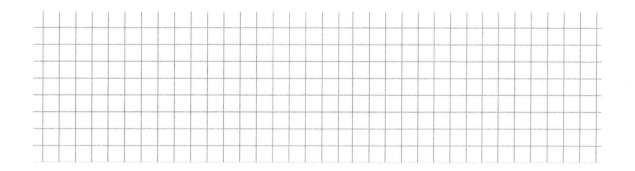

                                              Answer:_____

10. Write all the multiples of 17 below 100 in the correct region of the diagram below. "A" must contain all numbers which divide 255, while "B" must contain all numbers where the product of their digits is even (for example, if we consider 17, the product of its digits is 1 x 7 = 7).

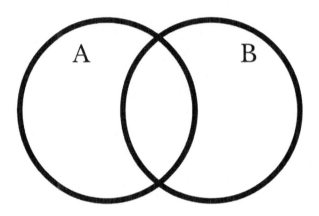

11. Sophie picks a letter at random from the following list:

A, B, R, W, W, Y, U, I, O, P, R, Q, E, R, I

a. Which letter is most likely to be picked?

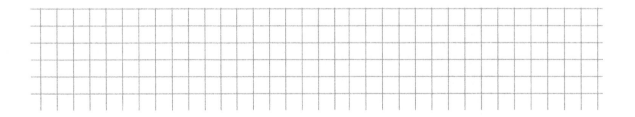

Answer:_____

b. Which letter has the same chance of being picked as W?

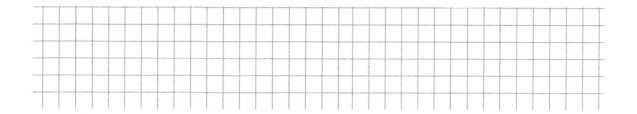

Answer:_____

12. The diagram below shows a regular octagon with a shaded region. What proportion of the octagon is shaded?

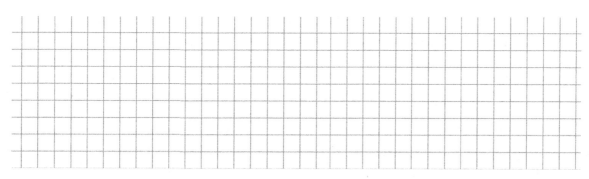

Answer:_____

13. a. On the axis below, mark the points (0,3) and (2,0).

b. Now plot their midpoint and write down its coordinate.

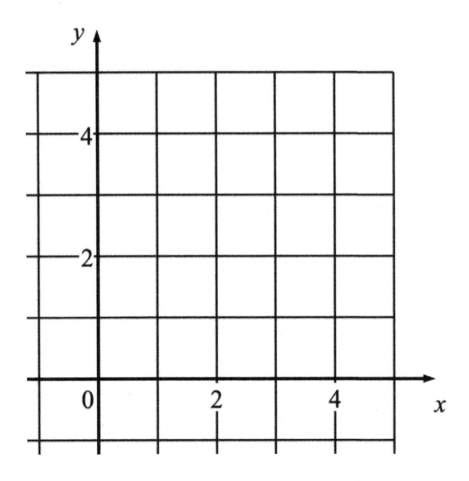

Answer:_____

14. Jim is working at a bowling alley, setting up the pins. He keeps making larger and larger pyramids as shown.

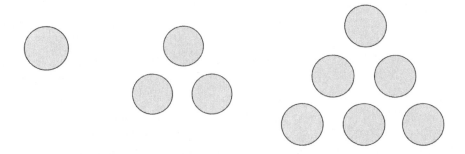

a. The diagram above shows 1, 2 and 3 rows of pins respectively. How many pins are required to build 7 rows of pins?

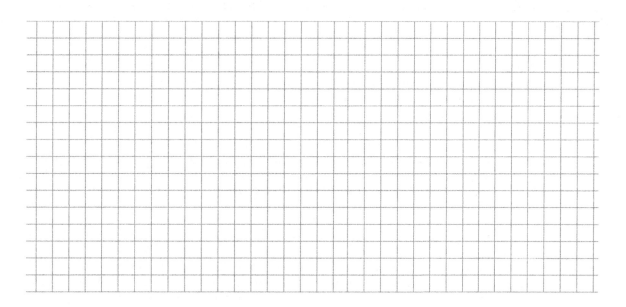

Answer:_____

b. If Jim wants to fill 8 bowling alleys with 5 rows of pins and 3 bowling alleys with 6 rows of pins, how many pins will he need in total?

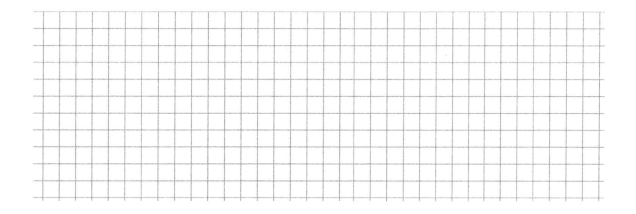

Answer:_____

15. The Number 11 tram leaves Station A every 13 minutes, passes through stations B, M, and N before returning to A. The 7 tram leaves Station A every 17 minutes, passes through stations C, T, and M, before returning to A. The 73a tram leaves Station A every 2 minutes, passes through stations V, X, and Tram interchange before returning to A.

a. All three trams leave Station A when the conductor blows his whistle at 10:00am. When is the first time all these trams will all leave station A at the same time again?

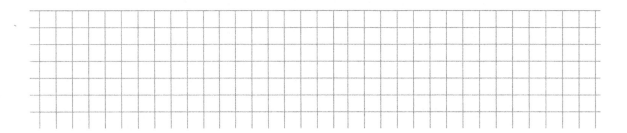

Answer:_____

b. On Tuesdays, all the trams must be back in at Station A by 5:00pm, and there is only one number 7 tram. How many laps will this tram make of its route on a Tuesday?

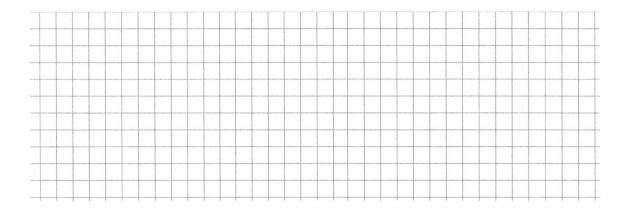

Answer:_____

16. Work out $(34-2) \div 8 + 3^2$

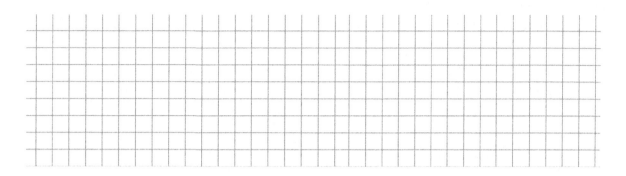

Answer:_____

17. If I draw a line between every two dots in the diagram below, how many lines will I have drawn?

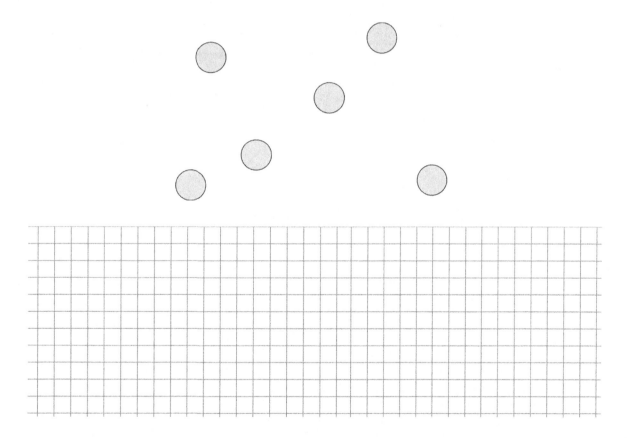

Answer:_____

18. Add the missing shape to each sequence

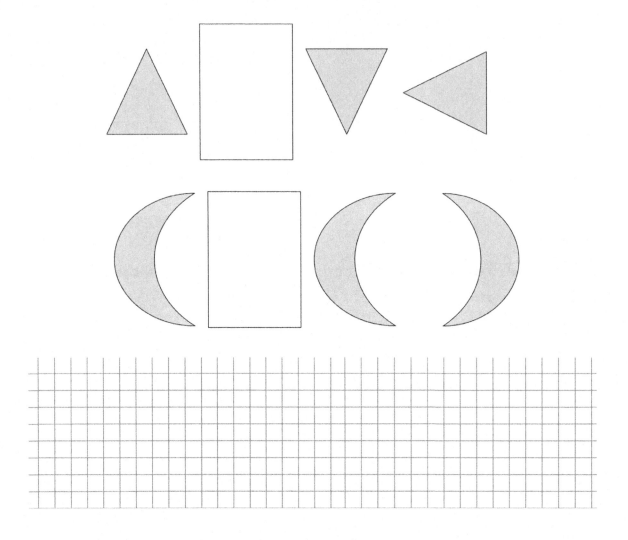

19. In 2022, June began on a Wednesday, what is the first day of November?

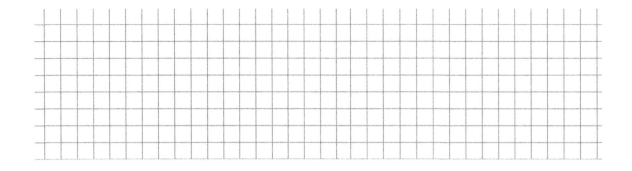

Answer:_____

20. Every number in this sequence is the average of the two beside it. Fill in the gaps.

3, ___, ___, 9, ___, 5, ___

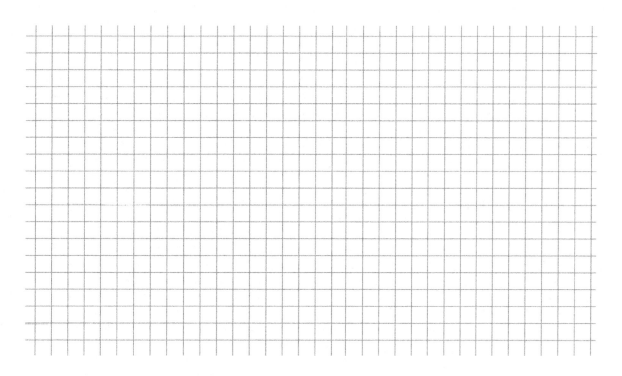

Answers and Guidance

1. Work out: 350 + 121 + 52

Take this in steps. First we do $121 + 52 = 173$, then we add the 350 to this, giving us:

$350 + 173 = \mathbf{523}$

Answer: 523

2. Work out: 34 x 56

Multiplication is easiest to break up into parts.

Notice that $34 = (30 + 4)$ and $56 = (50 + 6)$. Now we just need to multiply each term in either bracket together.

So $34 \times 56 = (30 + 4) \times (50 + 6) = (30 \times 50) + (4 \times 50) + (30 \times 6) + (4 \times 6)$

Then we just need to do the adding $1500 + 200 + 180 + 24 = \mathbf{1904}$

We could alternatively use the column method:

$$
\begin{array}{r}
3\overset{2}{4} \\
\times\ 56 \\
\hline
204 \\
+\ 1700 \\
\hline
1904
\end{array}
$$

Don't forget to add this extra zero here when multiplying by a two-digit number!

Answer: 1904

3. Work out: $20.1 \div 3$

Here we can use the classic bus stop method. First note that $20 \div 3$ is 6 with remainder 2.

Then we carry this 2 over to the .1, and note that $21 \div 3$ is 7. This gives the answer **6.7**.

$$
\begin{array}{r}
6.7 \\
3\overline{)2^{2}0.^{2}1}
\end{array}
$$

If you don't like the bus stop method, you can instead use the following chain of logic to glean the answer:

$$\frac{20.1}{3} = \frac{201}{30} = \frac{180}{30} + \frac{21}{30} = 6 + \frac{7}{10}$$

Answer: 6.7

4. Work out: -1 - 5.1

Don't get confused by the negative numbers here! Remember that -1 is smaller than 0, so when we take away 5.1, the result should be even smaller. You can think of subtracting from a negative number like adding, only the result is still negative. And so the answer is:

-1 - 5.1 = -(1 + 5.1) = -(6.1) = **-6.1**

Answer: -6.1

5. What are the missing terms in each of the following sequences:

a) 4, 10, ___, 22, 28, ___

b) ___, ___, 22, 18, 14

c) 1024, 512, 256, 128, ___, ___

d) 7, 4, 1, ___, ___

e) 1, 4, 9, 16, ___, ___

With sequences, the best approach is to look at the differences between the terms. The **difference** is the number you get when you subtract one number from another.

(a)

Take a) for example. 10 - 4 = 6 and 28 - 22 = 6, so it is sensible to assume that there is a difference of 6 between consecutive terms. So the answers are **16** and **34**.

Answer: 4, 10, 16, 22, 28, 34

(b)

In b), we notice that each term decreases by 4, so the answers are **30** and **26**.

Answer: 30, 26, 22, 18, 14

(c)

In c), we are required to notice that the terms are halving every time, so the answers are **64** and **32**.

Answer: 1024, 512, 256, 128, 64, 32

(d)

In d), note that not only are the terms decreasing, but they are allowed to decrease below 0 and become negative numbers; so the next terms are **-2** and **-5**.

Answer: 7, 4, 1, -2, -5

(e)

In e) we are required to notice that we are dealing with a familiar pattern of numbers: namely, the square numbers. The next two terms are then 5^2 = **25** and 6^2 = **36**.

Answer: 1, 4, 9, 16, <u>25</u>, <u>36</u>

6. Which of the numbers below are multiples of 74:

74	1	148
37	7474	370

A number is a multiple of 74 when division by 74 leaves no remainder. Obviously 74 is 1x74 so 74 ÷ 74 = 1 with no remainder.

1 and 37 are smaller than 74, so they can't be multiples.

148 is 2 x 74, so we know that 148 is a multiple of 74. And if we notice that 74 x 100 + 74 = 7400 + 74 = 7474, we can then infer that 74 x 101 = 7474.

Finally, we could use the bus stop method on 370 to show that it is divisible by 74. Alternatively, we could notice that 74 ÷ 2 = 37, and so 74 x 5 = 74 ÷ 2 x 10 = 37 x 10 = 370.

So the multiples of 74 are: **74**, **148**, **7474**, and **370**.

Answer: <u>74, 148, 7474, 370</u>

7. A train is travelling from Bristol to Norwich. The train leaves at 13:43pm and arrives at 00:13am.

a. How long is this journey in hours and minutes?

b. The distance from Bristol to Norwich is 210 miles. What is the speed of the train in mph?

(a)

When the journey crosses into the next day, we can split the problem into counting up to midnight, then adding the time after midnight. There are 10 hours until 23:43pm and then 17 minutes to 00:00am; finally we need to add the last 13 minutes to 00:13am.

Alternatively, we could've counted 11 hours forward to 00:43, and subtracted 30 minutes.

Either way, the answer is **10 hours 30 minutes**.

Answer: <u>10 hours 30 minutes</u>

(b)

For b), we note that we have travelled 210 miles in 10 hours and 30 minutes, so we need to figure out how many miles we went in 1 hour.

Since we have the distance (210 miles), and time taken ($10\frac{1}{2}$ hours), we simply need to do Speed = Distance ÷ Time.

That is:

$$Speed = \frac{210}{10.5} = \frac{2100}{105} = 20mph$$

So our answer is **20 mph**.

Answer: 20 mph

8. a. What is the mean, median and mode of the following list of numbers:

   8, 45, 6, 3, 1, 6, 3, 3, 15

b. Two other numbers are added to this list and the mean does not change. One is 19, what is the other number?

If you are not familiar with all these terms, we will give a definition of each below.

• The mean can be thought of as the average of a group of numbers. We can find this by adding all those numbers up, then dividing by the amount of numbers we have. So, as an example, if we have the heights of 6 boxes, that are 2m, 2m, 3m, 4m, 5m and 8m tall, then the mean height of all the boxes is:

(2+2+3+4+5+8) / 6 = 24 / 6 = 4m.

• The median is the middle value when we list the numbers in increasing order, so if we have the numbers 3, 4, 7, 2, 1, first we put them in increasing order:

1,2,3,4,7

...and then the middle number in this sequence is 3. Notice if we have 6 numbers instead of 5, there would be two numbers which sit in the middle; for example look at the sequence: 1,2,3,4,4,7. In this case we need to take the average (the mean) of the middle two numbers which are 3 and 4. The average of 3 and 4 is (3 + 4) / 2 = 3.5, so 3.5 is the median.

• The mode is quite simply the number that appears most frequently in a collection of numbers.

So, back to the question:

(a)

The best idea to start is to order the numbers 1, 3, 3, 3, 6, 6, 8, 15, 45. Then we can immediately see the **median is 6** and the **mode is 3**. The mean we can get from adding them all up and dividing by the number of numbers, that is:

$$\frac{90}{9} = 10$$

So our **mean is 10.**

Answer: Median: 6 | Mode: 3 | Mean: 10

(b)

When we add two more numbers, the number of numbers we have is 11, so for the mean to not change we need the new total to be 110. If our previous total was 90 and we add 19, this gives 109, and so the other number which was added to the list must be **1**.

So **1** is our answer.

Answer: <u>1</u>

9. Below you can see angles labelled on a triangle.

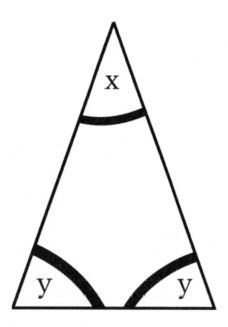

a. If x = 40, find y.

b. If x = 60, how many lines of symmetry does the triangle have?

(a)

We know that the angles in a triangle add up to 180°. So the size of the other two angles is (180 - 40) / 2 = **70** when x=40.

So **y = 70°**

Answer: <u>70°</u>

(b)

If x=60, then the other angles have size (180 - 60) / 2 = 60. So all the angles are equal and we have an equilateral triangle. Since all angles are equal (and so too is the length of each side), we have **three lines of symmetry** — draw the triangle if you're not convinced!

So our answer is **3 lines of symmetry**.

Answer: <u>3</u>

10. Write all the multiples of 17 below 100 in the correct region of the diagram below. "A" must contain all numbers which divide 255, while "B" must contain all numbers where the product of their digits is even (for example, if we consider 17, the product of its digits is 1 x 7 = 7).

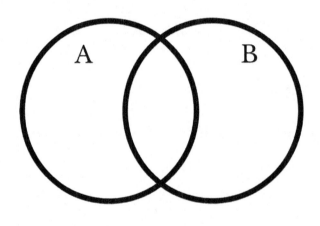

We first need to calculate all the multiples of 17 below 100, and there's not too many!

17, 34, 51, 68, 85. Note an easy way to do this quickly is add 20 and subtract 3 each time.

Then note that 5 x 51=255. This tells us that 51 belongs in category "A". We can also re-express this as 255 = 5 x (17 x 3), which tells us that 17 also belongs in "A". We also just recently established that 85 = 5 x 17. Putting this information together, we can say that 255 = (5 x 17) x 3 = 85 x 3, and thus 85 also goes in "A".

However, we know that 34 or 68 do *not* belong in "A" as 2 is not a prime factor of 255.

We can easily calculate the products of digits, or just note that the product of even numbers is even and the product of odd numbers is odd, which can save some time. The answer is shown in the diagram below:

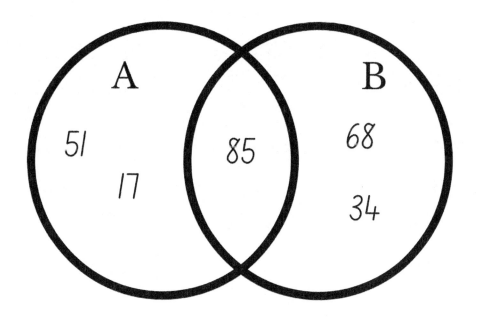

11. Sophie picks a letter at random from the following list:

A, B, R, W, W, Y, U, I, O, P, R, Q, E, R, I

a. Which letter is most likely to be picked?

b. Which letter has the same chance of being picked as W?

(a)

We are looking for the mode — that is, the most common value. Counting the frequency, we can see that **R** appears three times, which is more than any other letter. As such, the correct answer is **R**.

Answer: <u>R</u>

(b)

For the second question, we need a letter which is as common as W. The only other which occurs twice is <u>**I**</u>, which is our answer.

Answer: <u>I</u>

12. The diagram below shows a regular octagon with a shaded region. What proportion of the octagon is shaded?

Typically our objective here is to break the larger shape down into smaller ones. Notice that an octagon can be broken down into 8 equal regions as the next diagram shows.

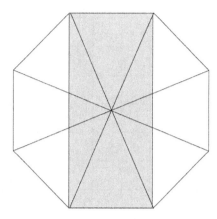

These 8 equal regions each comprise ⅛ of the total area.

Now, if we break one of these triangles in half, we have a smaller triangle that constitutes ¹/₁₆ of the total shape. And we can fit 8 of these smaller triangles into the shaded region:

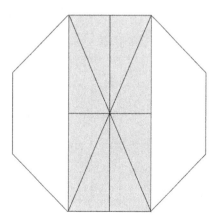

This gives us the answer:

$$8 \times \frac{1}{16} = \frac{1}{2}$$

So our answer is ½

Answer: ½ or 50% or 0.5 or half

13. On the axis below, mark the points (0,3) and (2,0).

Now plot their midpoint and write down its coordinate.

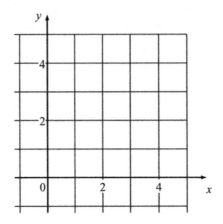

Crucial here is to remember that we are looking at the (x,y) coordinate, so we need to mark the point where x=0 and y=3, then x=2 and y=0, as shown below. To find the midpoint we just need the average of both coordinates. This is found at x = (0+2)/2 = 1 and y = (3+ 0)/2 = 1.5, which is also shown below.

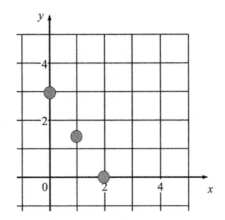

Midpoint coordinate: (1, 1.5)

14. Jim is working at a bowling alley, setting up the pins. He keeps making larger and larger pyramids as shown.

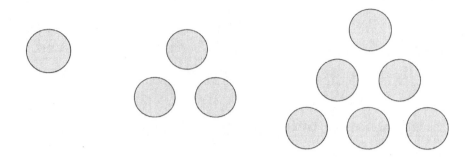

a. The diagram above shows 1, 2 and 3 rows of pins respectively. How many pins are required to build 7 rows of pins?

b. If Jim wants to fill 8 bowling alleys with 5 rows of pins and 3 bowling alleys with 6 rows of pins, how many pins will he need in total?

(a)

When Jim went from 1 row to 2 rows, he added 2 pins to the total; and when he went from 2 rows to 3, he added 3 more pins. It therefore follows that when Jim goes from 3 rows to 4 rows, he will need 4 more pins, so 6 + 4 = 10 pins in total. For 5 rows, he will need 5 more pins, so 15 in all; for 6 rows, Jim will require 21 pins; and for 7, he'll need **28**.

Answer: 28

(b)

Then for the second part we just need 8 x 15 + 3 x 21 = 120 + 63 = **183**

Answer: <u>183</u>

15. The Number 11 tram leaves Station A every 13 minutes, passes through stations B, M, and N before returning to A. The 7 tram leaves Station A every 17 minutes, passes through stations C, T, and M, before returning to A. The 73a tram leaves Station A every 2 minutes, passes through stations V, X, and Tram interchange before returning to A.

> **a. All three trams leave Station A when the conductor blows his whistle at 10:00am. When is the first time all these trams will all leave station A at the same time again?**
>
> **b. On Tuesdays, all the trams must be back in at Station A by 5:00pm, and there is only one number 7 tram. How many laps will this tram make of its route on a Tuesday?**

(a)

Here is a question which throws a lot of information at the reader when only a little of it is relevant. For the first part, we first want to work out the lowest common multiple (LCM) of the lap times of the 3 trams, that is 13, 17 and 2. Since 2, 13 and 17 are prime numbers, we know that their LCM is just 2 x 13 x 17 = 442.

We then need to figure out what time it is 442 minutes after 10:00am. Since 60 x 7 = 420, we first need to add on 7 hours, which takes us to 5pm. We then add on the spare 22 minutes, giving us 5:22pm

Answer: <u>5:22pm or 17:22</u>

(b)

For the second part, we first want to know how many minutes are in the time interval 10:00am to 5:00pm. This is a 7 hour period so we have 7 x 60 minutes = 420 minutes. Now we need the biggest multiple of 17 less than 420. Using the bus stop method we can find that 420 ÷ 17 is 24 remainder 12. So the answer is **24** — then the tram waits 12 minutes for the station to close!

Answer: <u>24</u>

16. Work out (34-2)÷8+3^2

This is simply a question of understanding the order of operations. Brackets, Indices, Division, Multiplication, Addition, Subtraction (BID-MAS). So let's do this in order

First, $(34-2)÷8+3^2 = (32)÷8+3^2 = 32÷8+9 = 4+9 = $ **13**.

So our answer is **13**.

Answer: <u>13</u>

17. If I draw a line between every two dots in the diagram below, how many lines will I have drawn?

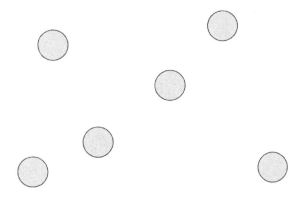

It may be easier to visualise this problem by rearranging the dots and a more ordered regular hexagon, and draw all the lines — or we can reason through it! Pick a point, then consider that it has to be connected to every other point with a line, so that's 5 lines. We have 6 points to pick so that makes 5x6 lines, but we have counted every line twice now, so we have to divide this by two. This gives (5x6)/2 = **15**.

Answer: 15

18. Add the missing shape to each sequence.

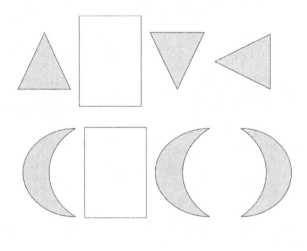

Usually there are only basic transformations, reflection or rotations, so don't over complicate things. The first one shows a rotation clockwise by 90 degrees, the second a reflection.

19. In 2022, June began on a Wednesday, what is the first day of November?

You will need some way of remembering how many days are in each month to pick up marks here. For reference June - 30, July - 31, August - 31, September - 30, October - 31, November - 30, December - 31. Then we simply need to calculate

30 + 31 + 31+ 30 + 31 = 153 and find the remainder of this when we divide by 7 which is 6. Thus the result is 6 days after Wednesday, which is **Tuesday**.

Answer: Tuesday

20. Every number in this sequence is the average of the two beside it. Fill in the gaps.

3, ___, ___, 9, ___, 5, ___

We can only work with what we are given, so let's start with the most straightforward gap, which is between 9 and 5. The average of 9 and 5 is $(9 + 5)/2 = 7$. Now we can fill in the gap to the left of 9 by finding a number x such that $(x + 7)/2 = 9$. If 7 is 2 less than 9, we need a number which is 2 more than 9 to balance this, so x = 11. Now we just need the average of 3 and 11 which is again 7; and finally we need the rightmost number, which, by the same logic as before, is 3.

Answer: 3, 7, 11, 9, 7, 5, 3

Exam Paper Two

60 Minutes | 20 Questions

Practice Paper Two
60 MINUTES: 20 QUESTIONS

1. Which of these fractions is the same a 1.2?

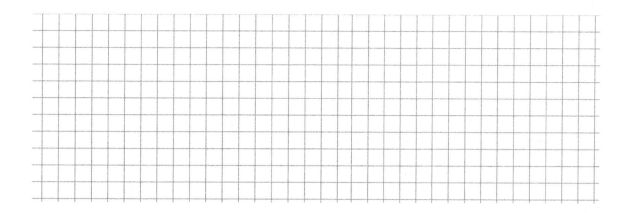

$$\frac{6}{5} \qquad \frac{1}{2}$$

$$\frac{1}{12} \qquad \frac{2}{1}$$

Answer:_____

2. I drop a ball from a height of 36cm, it hits the ground and bounces back up $\frac{1}{2}$ of its previous height. This happens 2 more times. What is the total distance the ball has travelled?

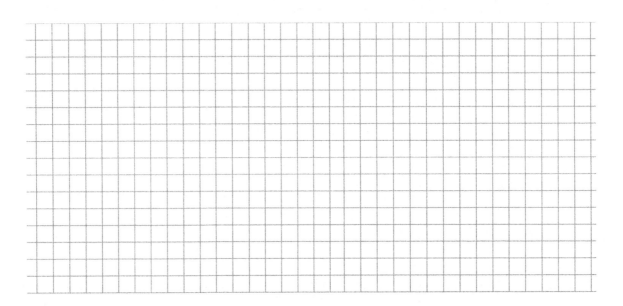

Answer:_____

3. Find the difference between 19435 when the digits are arranged in descending order, and 13630 when the digits are arranged in ascending order.

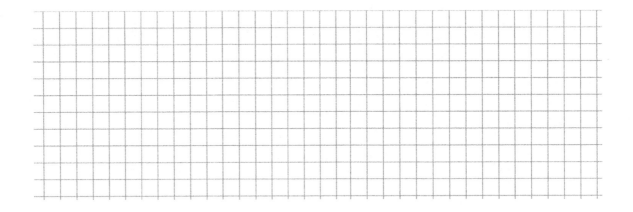

Answer:_____

4. I'm looking to buy a carpet for my living room. It must be 2m wide and 3m long to cover the floor, bright red, with purple spots. Jerry's Carpet Emporium is selling 6m² of such a carpet for 35% less than the label price of £200. How much would it cost me to cover my living room with this carpet?

Answer:_____

5. List all the numbers which are between 200 and 300, and have 2,3 and 11 as factors.

Answer:_____

6. I add 15 to a number then multiply by 7 and subtract 2, my answer is 96, what number did I start with?

Answer:_____

7. At the cinema I get a small bucket of popcorn, two large sodas and a chocolate bar, and the total cost of this is £6.74. If the chocolate bar costs £1.70 and a small bucket of popcorn and one large soda cost £4.02, how much does the small bucket of popcorn cost?

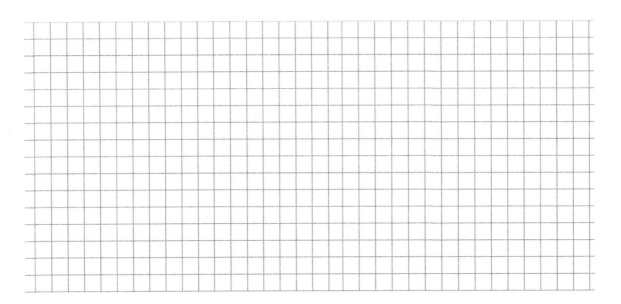

Answer:_____

8. If today is Wednesday and the time is 12:00pm, then how many seconds is it until next Wednesday at 12:00pm?

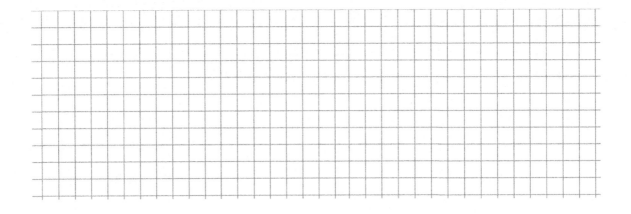

Answer:_____

9. Reflect each shaded square in the line shown in the diagram below.

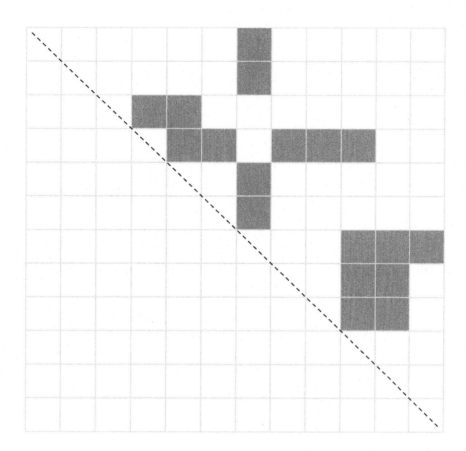

10. Write down 4 different multiples of 6 which add up to 96

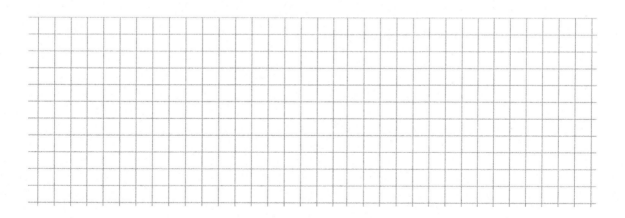

Answer:_____

11. What is the 76th letter in the sequence below

Q,W,E,R,T,Y,Q,W,E,R,T,Y,Q,W,E...

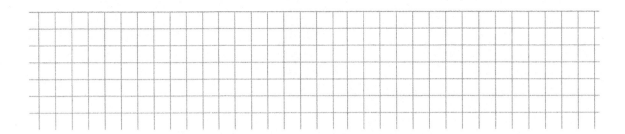

Answer:_____

12. If it takes four builders 4 hours to build a wall 4m high, how many builders does it take to build a wall 8m high in 4 hours?

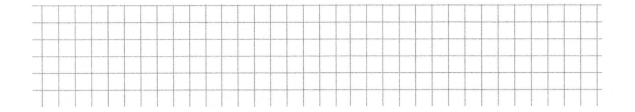

Answer:_____

13. I buy 6 bars of chocolate, and each one is £0.99. How much change do I get from a £20 note?

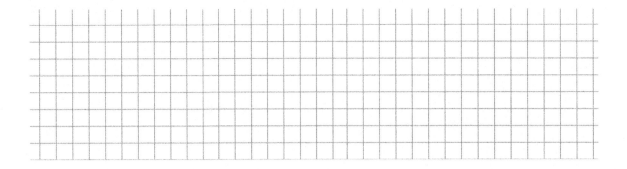

Answer:_____

14. a. The chart below shows the number of medals won by 4 nations at an international competition. Given the total number of medals handed out was 60, what is the number of medals the UK won?

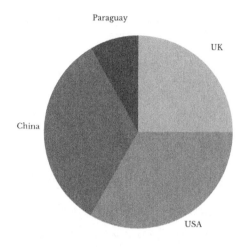

Answer:_____

b. Given the US won ⅓ of the medals, and China won the same amount as the US, how many medals did Paraguay win?

Answer:_____

15. Order these numbers from largest to smallest:

72.2   27.2   2.77   272   22.7   7.22   2.72

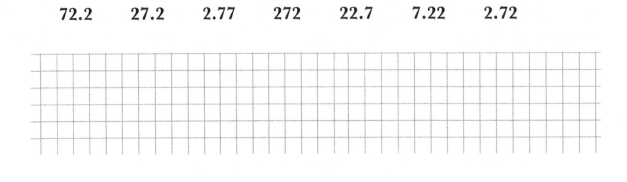

Answer:_____ _____ _____ _____ _____ _____ _____

16. My house number is 5 digits long, it starts with 8 and ends in 8. The third number is a multiple of 4. The sum of any 3 consecutive numbers in my house number is 20, what is the <u>only possible</u> house number I can have?

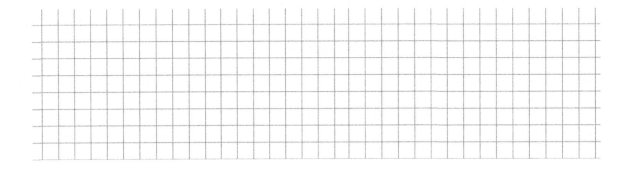

Answer:_____

17. Freddy counts the number of newts in a pond every day for 10 days, the results are:

3, 6, 6, 8, 9, 2, 2, 4, 6, 1

a. What's the mean number of newts Freddy saw across the 10-day period?

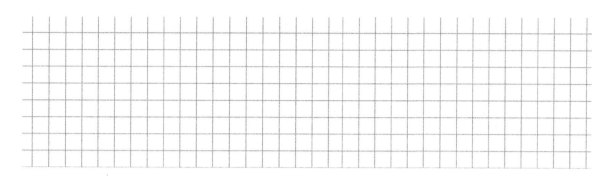

Answer:_____

b. Freddy further split the newts into two categories, red and blue tail, and counted how many there are of each he saw across the 10 day period. If the mean number of red tail newts he saw was 2.3 over the 10-day period, what was the total number of red tailed newts he saw?

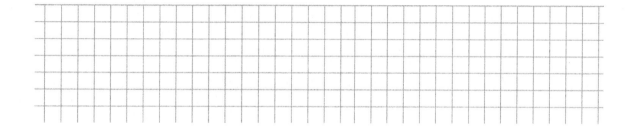

Answer:_____

c. What was the mean number of blue tail newts he saw?

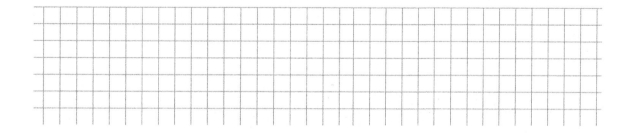

Answer:_____

18. In a bag there are twice as many red balls as blue balls, and there are 21 balls in total. How many red balls are there?

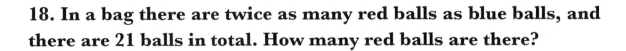

Answer:_____

19. Phil is on a train that left Bournemouth at 19:45, and is due to reach its final destination at 20:51. However, this train does not go direct from Bournemouth to its final stop; instead, it makes three other stops before the final destination, and there is an equal amount of time between each and every stop.

The time is currently 20:03. A group of passengers are being extremely loud, and Phil is deciding whether to change carriage. He decides that he will move if the group does not leave the train in the next 20 minutes. A person in the group says they are getting off at the stop after next.

Will Phil change carriage? Circle the correct answer.

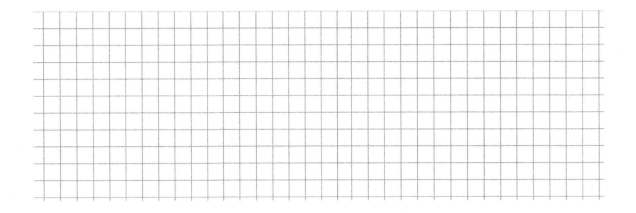

Answer: Yes / No

20. Given 1080 ÷ 12 = 90, find

a) 108 ÷ 12

Answer:_____

b) 1080 ÷ 48

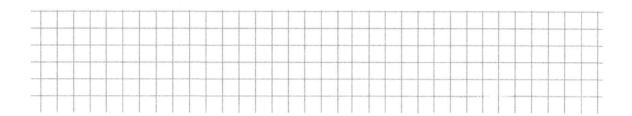

Answer:_____

c) 12 x 87

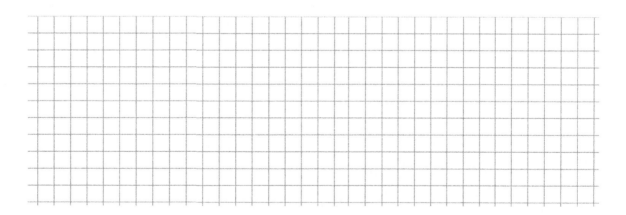

Answer:_____

d) 91 x 11

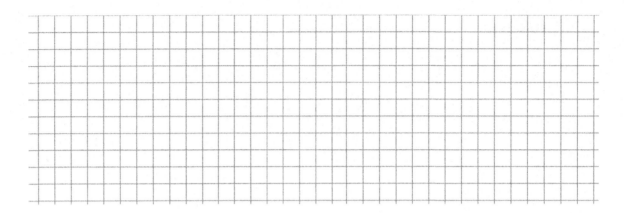

Answer:_____

Answers and Guidance

1. Which of these fractions is the same a 1.2?

$\dfrac{6}{5}$	$\dfrac{1}{2}$
$\dfrac{1}{12}$	$\dfrac{2}{1}$

We can eliminate ½ and ¹⁄₁₂ as they are both less than 1. Clearly ²⁄₁ is 2, so the answer must be ⁶⁄₅.

Answer: ⁶⁄₅

2. I drop a ball from a height of 36cm, it hits the ground and bounces back up ½ of its previous height. This happens 2 more times. What is the total distance the ball has travelled?

We just need to understand that every time the ball bounces back up half the height of last time. So the first time we bounce back to a height of 18, the second time to a height of 9, and the last time to a height of 4.5. So, since we finish at the top, the total distance travelled is 36 + 18 x 2 + 9 x 2 + 4.5 , this sum is **94.5**.

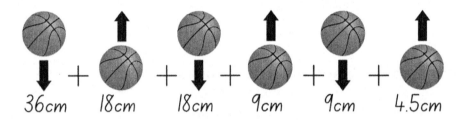

Answer: 94.5

3. Find the difference between 19435 when the digits are arranged in descending order, and 13630 when the digits are arranged in ascending order.

First we arrange the digits: we have 95431 for the first set of digits, and 01336 for the second. Don't get confused by the second number: this is just a 4 digit number now. The difference is:

95431 - 1336 = **94095**

Answer: 94095

4. I'm looking to buy a carpet for my living room. It must be 2m wide and 3m long to cover the floor, bright red, with purple spots. Jerry's Carpet Emporium is selling 6m^2 of such a carpet for 35% less than the label price of £200. How much would it cost me to cover my living room with this carpet?

Since the surface area I need to cover is 2x3m = 6 m^2, we only need to find 35% of 200.

We can either get 5% by noticing that 5% = 0.05 = $^1/_{20}$, so 5% of 200 is $^{200}/_{20}$ = 10, then multiply by 7. Alternatively, we could note that 35% of 100 is 35, and then multiply this by 2.

Either way our answer is 70. This is the discount applied to the original price of £200, so I end up paying 200-70= **£130**.

Answer: £130

5. List all the numbers which are between 200 and 300, and have 2,3 and 11 as factors.

Since 2, 3 and 11 are all prime, their LCM is just the product 2 x 3 x 11 = 66. So we know that every number which has these numbers as factors is a multiple of 66. So there is a gap of 66 between each number we are looking for.

Notice 66 x 2 = 132, and 66 x 3 = 132 + 66 = 198. Then we can quickly get 66 x 4 = 132 x 2 = 264. We could also would out 5 x 66 as 132 + 198, (or (66 x 10) ÷ 2) but we don't need to, since we already know the gaps between numbers are 66 and clearly 264 + 66 > 300; so we know the only answer is **264**.

Answer: <u>264</u>

6. I add 15 to a number then multiply by 7 and subtract 2, my answer is 96, what number did I start with?

We clearly need to work backwards and just not get confused. Everywhere we see a subtraction we change it to an addition, and everywhere we multiplication we swap it with a division. We work backward through the sentence 96 + 2 = 98; 98 ÷ 7 = 14; 14 - 15 = -1. So the answer is **-1**.

Answer: <u>-1</u>

7. At the cinema I get a small bucket of popcorn, two large sodas and a chocolate bar, and the total cost of this is £6.74. If the chocolate bar costs £1.70 and a small bucket of popcorn and one large soda cost £4.02, how much does the small bucket of popcorn cost?

First we can deduct the cost of the chocolate bar from the total. £6.74 - £1.70 = £5.04. Since we know the cost of one soda and one popcorn (£4.02), and the cost of two soda and one popcorn (£5.04), their difference must be exactly the price of one soda, so one soda costs £5.04 - £4.02 = £1.02. This means we can work out the popcorn costs: £4.02- £1.02 = **£3**.

Answer: <u>£3</u>

8. If today is Wednesday and the time is 12:00pm, then how many seconds is it until next Wednesday at 12:00pm?

This time interval is exactly 7 days, or one week. So we just need to work out how many seconds there are in a week. This is just a multiplication. We have 60 seconds in a minute, 60 minutes in an hour, 24 hours in a day and 7 days in a week. So we need to find 60 x 60 x 24 x 7. Let's do this in parts. 60 x 60 = 3600, and 24 x 7 = 20 x 7 + 4 x 7 = 140 + 28 = 168.

Then: 3 x 168 = 3 x 100 + 3 x 60 + 3 x 8 = 300 + 180 + 24 = 504.

So we can quickly get: 6 x 168 = 2 x 3 x 168 = 2 x 504 = 1008

So 168 x 3600 = 168 x 3000 + 168 x 600 = 504000 + 100800 = **604800**.

You could also use the column method to tackle these multiplications, if you find it more simple.

Answer: 604800

9. Reflect each shaded square in the line shown in the diagram below.

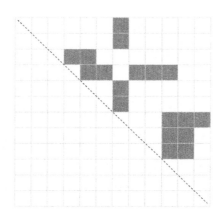

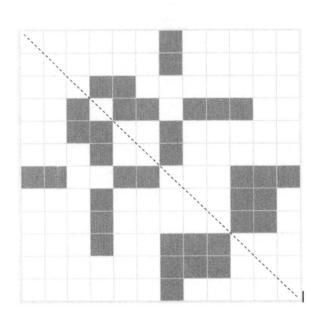

10. Write down 4 different multiples of 6 which add up to 96

We could do this by trial and error, as there are only 15 different multiples of 6 less than 96.

Or we could notice that 96= 6 x 16 = 6 x (1+4+5+6) = 6x1 + 6x4 + 6x5 + 6x6. So one potential answer is 6 + 24 + 30 + 36.

Indeed, if we take any four digits that add up to 16, and then multiply each of those numbers by 6, you will have four new digits that together add up to 96, so there are in fact many possible answers!

A potential correct answer: 6, 24, 30, 36
Another potential correct answer: 6, 12, 18, 60

11. What is the 76th letter in the sequence below:

Q,W,E,R,T,Y,Q,W,E,R,T,Y,Q,W,E...

First we notice the pattern, the sequence repeats every 6 characters, Q,W,E,R,T,Y. This means the 1st letter will be the same as the 7th letter and the 13th letter, etc. The same is true for the 2nd letter, 8th letter, 14th letter. If we take any number, and find its remainder when dividing by 6, we can work out the corresponding letter in the sequence. If the remainder is 2, then it will be the same as the 2nd letter in the sequence. $76 \div 6$ is 12 with remainder 4, so we need the 4th letter in the sequence, so the answer is **R**.

Answer: <u>R</u>

12. If it takes four builders 4 hours to build a wall 4m high, how many builders does it take to build a wall 8m high in 4 hours?

We need to do twice as much work in the same amount of time, so logically we need twice as many people to achieve this. We can also directly calculate that four builders in one hour build one quarter of the wall, so this wall will be 1m high. So each builder builds 0.25m of wall per hour. So if we have **<u>8 builders</u>** we are building $8 \times 0.25 = 2$m every hour, so in 4 hours we will have built a wall 8m high.

A side note: some of you may have been distracted by some more real world concerns. Is it *really* the case that doubling the amount of builders doubles the output? What if the builders spent the first hour waiting for the bricks to arrive, or the last hour for the cement to set? In the real world, doubling workers doesn't always lead to double efficiency. However, it's important to remember that we can only work with the information we have been given, so it's important to suspend disbelief and work with what we have — in other words, to see past the setting of the problem to the maths question behind it.

Similar questions to this — that is, questions that require us to ignore 'real world concerns' — have come up before in 11+ paper, so make sure you don't get distracted. Instead, simply focus on the maths!

Answer: <u>8</u>

13. I buy 6 bars of chocolate, and each one is £0.99. How much change do I get from a £20 note?

We could calculate 99 x 6, but to save time let's do 100 x 6 and subtract 6, in other words 99 x 6 = (100 - 1) x 6 = 600 - 6 = 594. So we need £20.00 - £5.94 = **£14.06**.

Answer: <u>£14.06</u>

14. a. The chart below shows the number of medals won by 4 nations at an international competition. Given the total number of medals handed out was 60, what is the number of medals the UK won?

b. Given the US won ⅓ of the medals, and China won the same amount as the US, how many medals did Paraguay win?

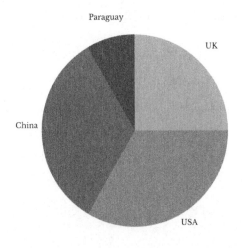

(a)

First we must observe visually that the UK makes up ¼ of the pie chart, as the UK section makes a right angle. So the UK won 60 ÷ 4 = **15 medals**.

Answer: 15

(b)

We can get the second answer by finding ⅓ of 60 which is 20; then since we know that the UK, China and the US won a total of 20 + 20 + 15 = 55 medals, we know also that Paraguay must have won **5**.

Answer: 5

15. Order these numbers from largest to smallest:

72.2   27.2   2.77   272   22.7   7.22   2.72

There's not much more to say other than: know your decimals, and make sure you are going from largest to smallest. And be careful: this is an easy place to lose easy marks! The answer is **272, 72.2, 27.2, 22.7, 7.22, 2.77, 2.72.**

Answer: 272, 72.2, 27.2, 22.7, 7.22, 2.77, 2.72

16. My house number is 5 digits long, it starts with 8 and ends in 8. The third number is a multiple of 4. The sum of any 3 consecutive numbers in my house number is 20, what is the *only possible* house number I can have?

We first have to notice there are only two possibilities for the middle number, either 4 or 8.

If the middle number is 4, then 8+4 is 12 so the second number must be 8. The same calculation shows the fourth number is 8. So this gives **88488**. The sum of the second, third and fourth numbers is $8 + 4 + 8$, so this is a valid house number.

If the middle number is 8, then by the same logic the second and fourth numbers are both 4, but then the sum of the middle numbers is $4 + 8 + 4 = 16$

Answer: <u>88488</u>

17. Freddy counts the number of newts in a pond every day for 10 days. The results are:

3, 6, 6, 8, 9, 2, 2, 4, 6, 1

a. What's the mean number of newts Freddy saw across the 10-day period?

b. Freddy further split the newts into two categories, red and blue tail, and counted how many there are of each he saw across the 10 day period. If the mean number of red tail newts he saw was 2.3 over the 10-day period, what was the total number of red tailed newts he saw?

c. What was the mean number of blue tail newts he saw?

(a)

First we work out the mean. The sum of the numbers is 47, so their mean is **4.7**.

Answer: <u>4.7</u>

(b)

Now we have to think about *how* the mean is calculated for the second part. If the mean number of red tail newts was 2.3 over 10 days, then we know that the total number, which we will call "X", needs to be such that X ÷ 10 = 2.3; so obviously the total is <u>**23**</u>.

Answer: 23

(c)

To find the mean number of blue tail newts, we just need the total Freddy saw, which is 47-23 = 24. Then we divide this by the number of days, 10, to get **2.4**.

Answer: <u>2.4</u>

<u>18. In a bag there are twice as many red balls as blue balls, and there are 21 balls in total. How many red balls are there?</u>

This is really a ratio question in disguise, the ratio of red balls to blue balls is 2:1, so a third of the balls are blue. Thus, there are 7 blue balls, and so there are **14 red balls**.

Answer: <u>14</u>

19. Phil is on a train that left Bournemouth at 19:45, and is due to reach its final destination at 20:51. However, this train does not go direct from Bournemouth to its final stop; instead, it makes three other stops before the final destination, and there is an equal amount of time between each and every stop.

The time is currently 20:03. A group of passengers are being extremely loud, and Phil is deciding whether to change carriage. He decides that he will move if the group does not leave the train in the next 20 minutes. A person in the group says they are getting off at the stop after next.

Will Phil change carriage?

There's a lot of information to unpack here. We need to work out if the group will leave before Phil's deadline.

First let's figure out when each stop happens. The difference between 19:45 and 20:51 is 66 minutes. We know Phil's is the fourth and final stop, and so there are 4 equal intervals of 16 minutes and 30 seconds between each stop.

The time is 20:03, which is 18 minutes after the departure time, so the train has already cleared one station. The next stop will be at 20:18, and the stop after that — which is when the group will be leaving — will be just after 20:34. This is more than 31 minutes from the current time

(22:03). This is well after Phil's deadline of 20 minutes, **so he will indeed change carriage**.

Answer: <u>**Yes, Phil will change carriages.**</u>

20. Given 1080 ÷ 12 = 90, find

a) 108 ÷ 12

b) 1080 ÷ 48

c) 12 x 87

d) 91 x 11

These are all questions you could solve without the hint, but since we've been given information, let's use it!

(a)

If we know $1080 \div 12 = 90$ it is a sensible guess that $108 \div 12 = \underline{\mathbf{9}}$, we can see this is true by writing:

$$108 \div 12 = {}^{108}/_{12} = {}^{108}/_{12} \times 1 = {}^{108}/_{12} \times {}^{10}/_{10} = {}^{108}/_{12} \times 10 \times {}^{1}/_{10} = {}^{108 \times 10}/_{12} \times {}^{1}/_{10}$$
$$= 90 \times {}^{1}/_{10} = 9$$

Alternatively, we can derive this same answer using our 12 times table. However, the reasoning used above will help us with the next answers…

Answer: <u>9</u>

(b)

We also know $1080 \div 48 = {}^{1080}/_{48} = {}^{1080}/_{12} \times \frac{1}{4} = 90 \times \frac{1}{4} = \mathbf{15}$

Answer: <u>**15**</u>

(c)

For the multiplication questions we can note that

$12 \times 87 = 12 \times (90 - 3) = 12 \times 90 - 12 \times 3 = 1080 - 36 = \mathbf{1044}$.

Answer: <u>**1044**</u>

(d)

And $91 \times 11 = (90 + 1) \times (12 - 1) = 90 \times 12 + 12 - 90 - 1 = 1080 + 12 - 91 = \mathbf{1001}$.

Answer: <u>**1001**</u>

Exam Paper Three

60 Minutes | 20 Questions

Practice Paper Three

1. A concert hall has 10 rows of 8 seats at the front, and a further 5 rows of 13 seats. The seats are numbered from left to right and from front to back, with the numbers 1 to 145. Each row is lettered, with A being the first row from the front, B the second etc.

If my seat number is 112, what is the letter of my row?

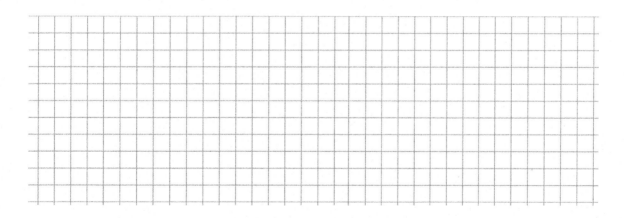

Answer:_____

2. Draw all (if any) lines symmetry on the following shapes.

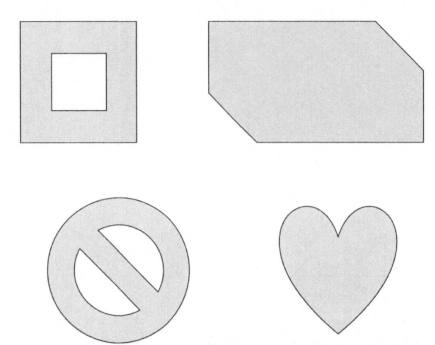

3. Which of the following statements is true?

   a) **8% of 15 is bigger than 15% of 8**

   b) **15% of 8 is bigger than 8% of 15**

   c) **8% of 15 is equal to 15% of 8**

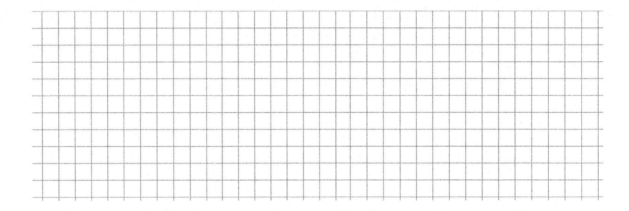

Answer:_____

4. What is the highest common factor of 238 and 168?

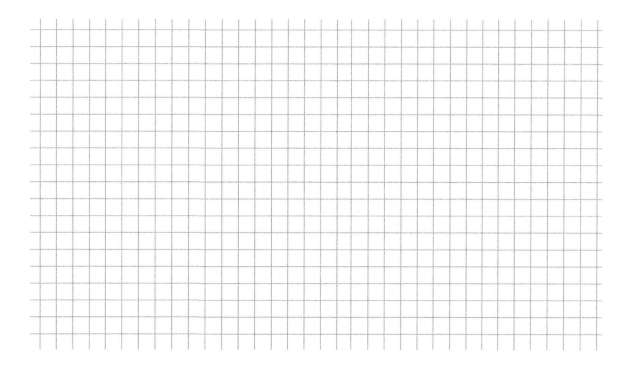

Answer:_____

5. Circle the most sensible unit to measure the following:

The mass of my cousin

grams   kilograms   tonnes

The speed of a train

kps   kpm   kph

6. Michael, Daniel and Max are standing on boxes which are 1.5, 2.3 and 0.7 metres high respectively. Priyansh measures the distance from the top of their heads to the ground when on the boxes. The results are given in the table below

Person	Measurement
Michael	3.1 Metres
Daniel	4 Metres
Max	2.2 Metres

a) What is the average height of the boxes?

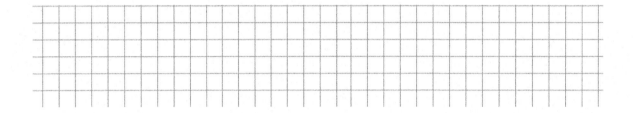

Answer:_____

b) The three boys get off their boxes. What is their average height?

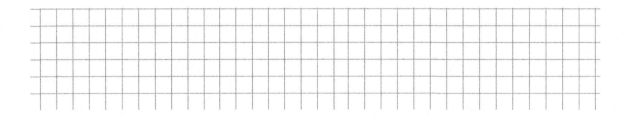

Answer:_____

7. The diagram shows a shape formed of regular pentagons called a pentaring, where the edges of each pentagon meet perfectly, such that the vertices of both ends of each shared edge touch.

Given that the side length of each pentagon is 5cm, what is the perimeter of the pentaring?

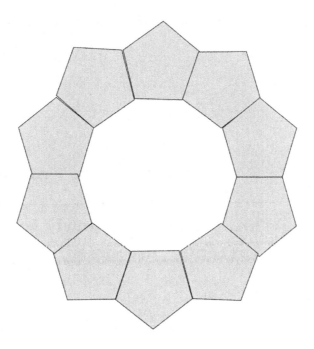

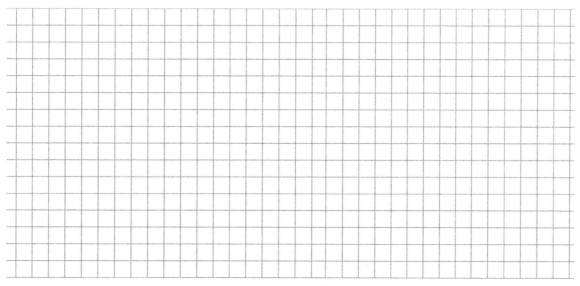

Answer:_____

8. Red Rum is a horse who walks 5km in 1 hour. Mike the donkey is ⅓ as fast as Red Rum. How long will it take Mike to walk 5km?

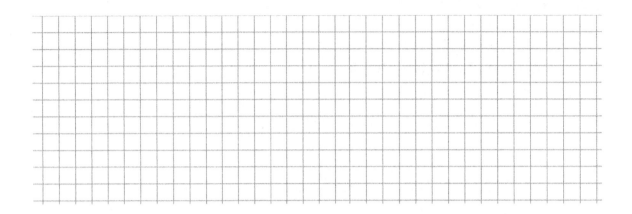

Answer:_____

9. My shop, Reggie's Discounts, previously sold lemonade for 92p per bottle, but I recently discounted the price to 55p per bottle.

If I sell 150 bottles of lemonade in the next 4 days at this discounted price, how much less money would I make compared to selling the same number of bottles at the original price? Give your answer in pounds and pence.

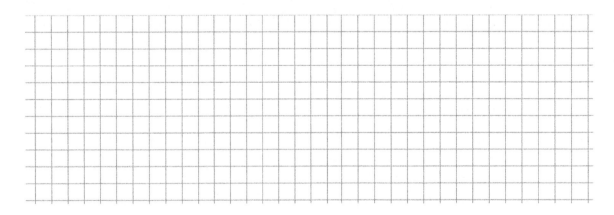

Answer:_____

10. What are the missing prime numbers?

41, 43, ?, ?, 59

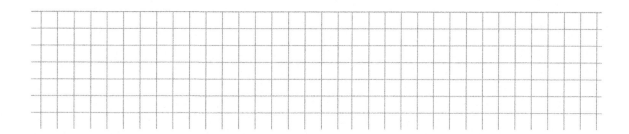

Answer:_____

11. a. Write down the value of these Roman numerals:

- **V**
- **L**

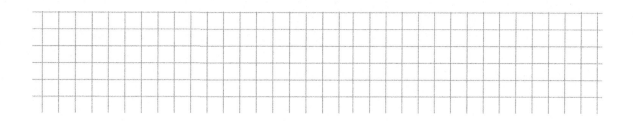

V:_____
L:_____

c. What year is written in Roman numerals as MMXIV?

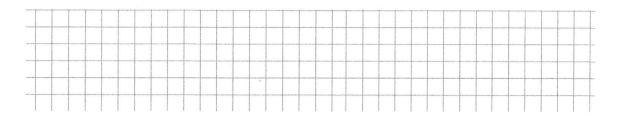

Answer:_____

12. Write 90 as a product of its prime factors.

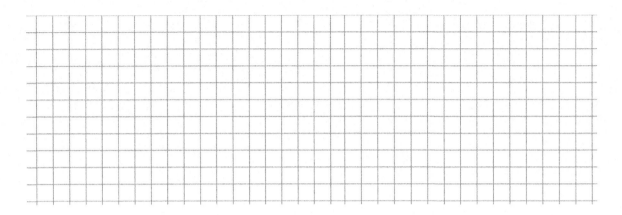

Answer:_____

13. In the sequence 3, 4, 6, 10, 18, ... what is the first three digit number that appears?

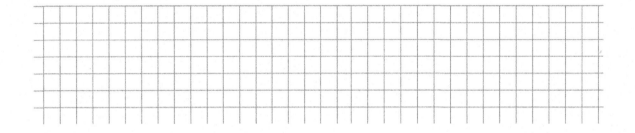

Answer:_____

14. Which name best describes the below shape? Circle the correct answer.

- Prism
- Pyramid
- Heptadecagon

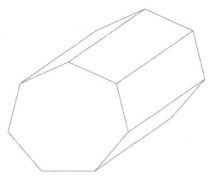

15. a. Label North, East, South, and West on the compass below.

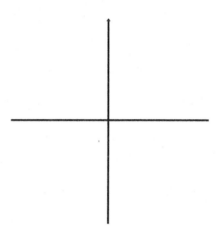

b. If I am facing East, and turn 125 degrees clockwise 3 times, then a further 75 degrees, which direction am I facing?

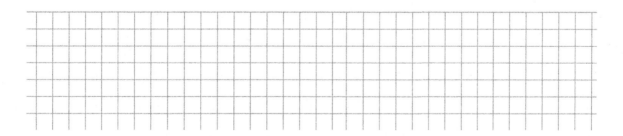

Answer:_____

16. Consider the diagram below. Lines MN and PQ are parallel.

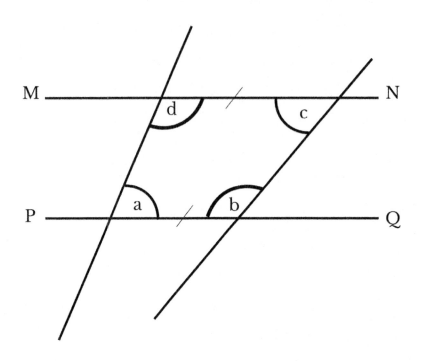

a. If a = 70, what is d?

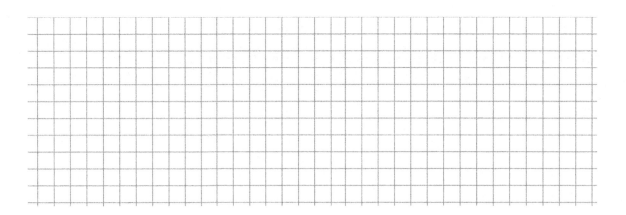

Answer:_____

b. Now we change b and c to right angles (as can be seen in the diagram below). If a = 70, what is d?

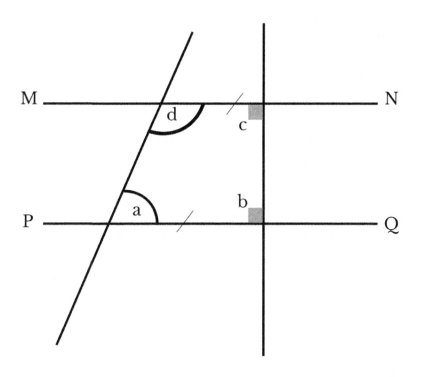

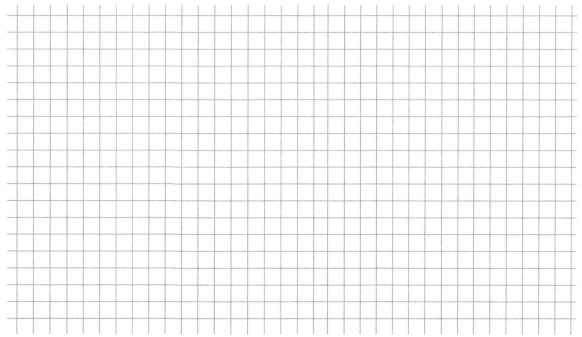

Answer:_____

c. Given the last two examples, if I have a new line crossing MN and PQ, what must be the sum of angles x and y?

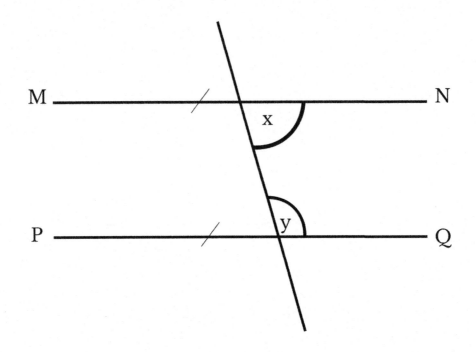

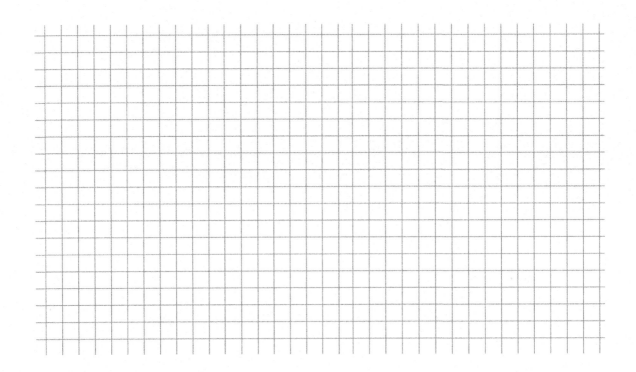

Answer:_____

17. Simplify the following ratios

a) 42 : 6

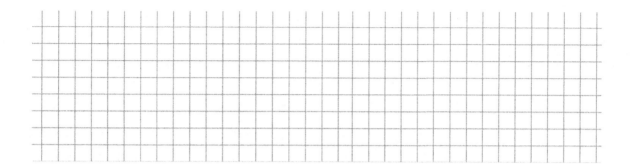

Answer:_____

b) 15 : 35

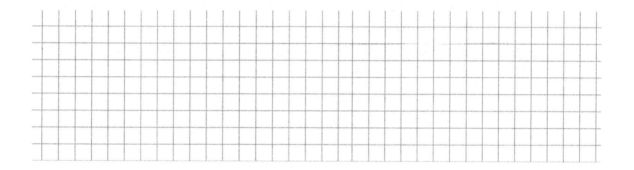

Answer:_____

c) 6 : 22

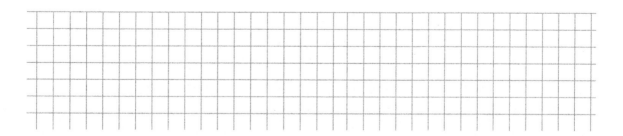

Answer:_____

18. In Oslo the temperature is -15C and in Berlin it is 11C. How much warmer is it in Berlin than in Oslo?

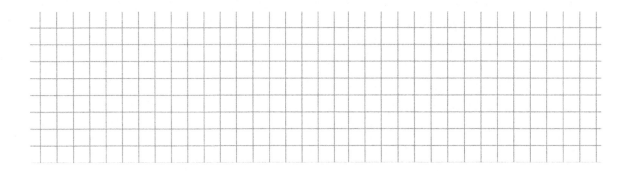

Answer:_____

19. Two numbers, A and B, have two distinct prime factors each, neither of which they have in common. Their difference is 1. They are both less than 22. A is bigger than B. What is B?

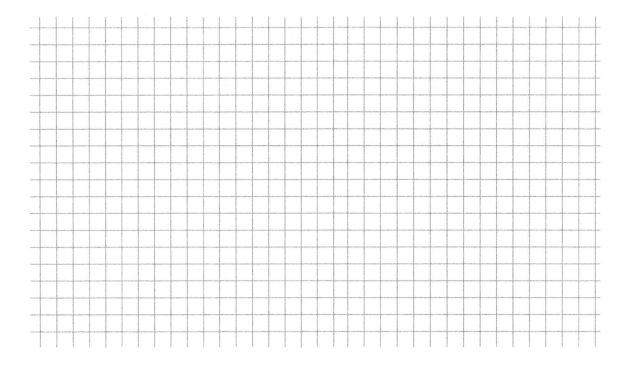

Answer:_____

20. If I am 90 years, 80 months, 70 weeks and 60 days old today, how many complete years have I lived?

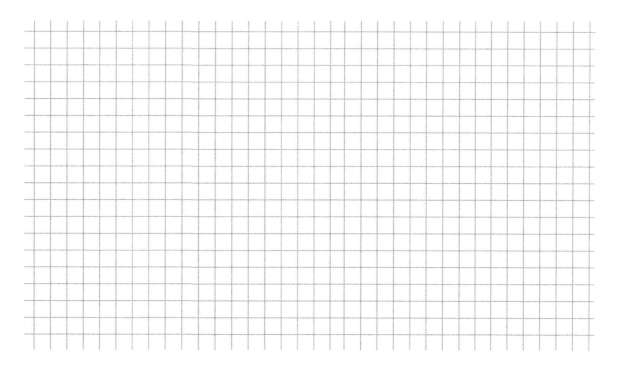

Answer:_____

Answers and Guidance

1. A concert hall has 10 rows of 8 seats at the front, and a further 5 rows of 13 seats. The seats are numbered from left to right and from front to back, with the numbers 1 to 145. Each row is lettered, with A being the first row from the front, B the second etc.

If my seat number is 112, what is the letter of my row?

The first 10 rows make up the first 1 to 80 seats, so we just need to keep adding 13 until we get a number higher than 112. Adding 13 several times over we get 93, 106, 119. So my seat is in the 10+ 3 = 13th row. The 13th letter of the alphabet is M, so I am in row **M**.

Answer: <u>M</u>

2. Draw all (if any) lines symmetry on the following shapes.

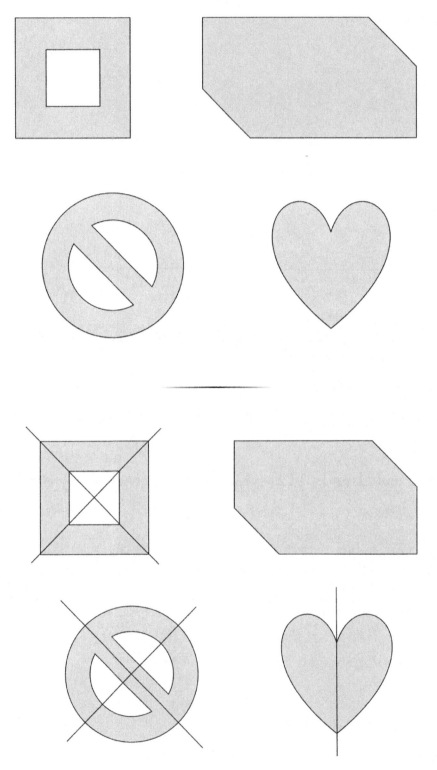

Don't be afraid to also identify that there are no lines of symmetry in the top right!

3. Which of the following statements is true?

    a) 8% of 15 is bigger than 15% of 8

    b) 15% of 8 is bigger than 8% of 15

    c) 8% of 15 is equal to 15% of 8

The correct answer is (c). You might find this surprising, but it is always true when we reverse the numbers in this way. We can see it more clearly if we convert the numbers into fractions:

$$8\% \text{ of } 15 = 15 \times \tfrac{8}{100} = \tfrac{15 \times 8}{100} = \tfrac{8 \times 15}{100} = 8 \times \tfrac{15}{100} = 15\% \text{ of } 8$$

Answer: C

4. What is the highest common factor of 238 and 168?

We'll need the prime factorisations of both 168 and 238. Let's start with the smaller, as this can often help in the process of finding the prime factorisation of the bigger.

$$168 = 2 \times 84 = 2 \times 2 \times 42 = 2 \times 2 \times 2 \times 21 = 2^3 \times 3 \times 7$$

Now we need the prime factors of 238. 2 is clearly a prime factor and we can note that $238 = 2 \times 119$.

Note that it is quite obvious 3 is not a divisor of 119, since 3 is a divisor of 120, and this can also be confirmed with the bus stop method. So we only have to check whether 7 is a divisor. Using the bus stop method, we find $119 = 17 \times 7$.

As 17 is prime, we are done and can identify the highest common factor (HCF) by the prime factors which 238 and 168 share, which here is only 2 and 7. Thus the HCF is **14.**

Bonus: When finding the prime factorisation of 238, we could've been really clever and noted that:

$238 = 168 + 70 = 2^3 \times 3 \times 7 + 10 \times 7 = (2^3 \times 3 + 10) \times 7 = (21 + 10) \times 7 = 34 \times 7$, which is a much quicker route.

Answer: 14

5. Circle the most sensible unit to measure the following:

a. The mass of my cousin

grams   kilograms   tonnes

b. The speed of a train

kps   kpm   kph

(a)

For the first question, we need to realise that nobody's cousin weighs one tonne (which is 1,000 kilograms). Grams would also not be wise, as most humans weigh more than a kilogram. So the answer is **kilograms**.

Answer: kilograms

(b)

For the second, we can start by noting that no train is able to move a kilometre in either a second or a minute. As such, **kilometres per hour (kph)** is the sensible choice.

Answer: <u>kilometres per hour (kph)</u>

<u>6. Michael, Daniel and Max are standing on boxes which are 1.5, 2.3 and 0.7 metres high respectively. Priyansh measures the distance from the top of their heads to the ground when on the boxes. The results are given in the table below.</u>

Person	Measurement
Michael	3.1 Metres
Daniel	4 Metres
Max	2.2 Metres

<u>a. What is the average height of the boxes?</u>

<u>b. The three boys get off their boxes. What is their average height?</u>

(a)

To find the average height of the boxes we just need $(1.5 + 2.3 + 0.7) / 3 =$ $4.5/3 =$ **1.5.**

Answer: 1.5 metres

(b)

For the average height of the people once they're off the boxes, we could subtract each box height from the right entry in the table, $3.1 - 1.5 = 1.6$, $4 - 2.3 = 1.7$, $2.2 - 0.7 = 1.5$. The average of these three values is $(1.6 + 1.7 + 1.5) / 3 =$ **1.6m**.

Alternatively we could skip the step of subtracting each value, by taking the average of the measurements, $(3.1 + 4 + 2.2) / 3 = 9.3 / 3 = 3.1$ and subtract the average height of the boxes, $3.1 - 1.5 = 1.6$.

Answer: 1.6 metres

7. The diagram shows a shape formed of regular pentagons called a pentaring, where the edges of each pentagon meet perfectly, such that the vertices of both ends of each shared edge touch.

Given that the side length of each pentagon is 5cm, what is the perimeter of the pentaring?

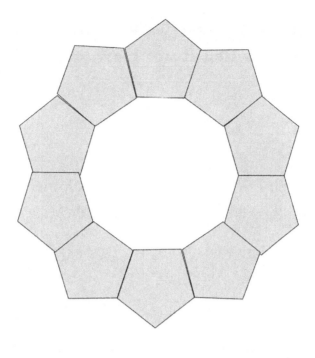

We can work out the perimeter of the shape's interior — that is, the outer-edges of the white shape within the pentaring — and add it to the perimeter of the exterior of the pentaring. There are 10 sides of the interior and 20 sides on the exterior, and each are 5cm long, so we need:

10 x 5 + 20 x 5 = **150cm.**

Alternatively we could note that each pentagon shares two sides with another shape, so these two sides are not counted in the total perimeter. That means that each pentagon contributes 3 x 5cm = 15cm to the total perimeter. There are 10 pentagons, so the total perimeter is 15cm x 10 = 150cm.

Answer: <u>150cm</u>

8. Red Rum is a horse who walks 5km in 1 hour. Mike the donkey is ⅓ as fast as Red Rum. How long will it take Mike to walk 5km?

First we need to establish Mike's speed in kph (kilometres per hour). If Red Rum walks at 5 kph, then Mike walks at 5/3 kph.

Since Mike walks 5/3 km each hour, we can extrapolate that it will take Mike **3 hours** to walk 5km.

Answer: 3 Hours

9. My shop, Reggie's Discounts, previously sold lemonade for 92p per bottle, but I recently discounted the price to 55p per bottle.

If I sell 150 bottles of lemonade in the next 4 days at this discounted price, how much less money would I make compared to selling the same number of bottles at the original price? Give your answer in pounds and pence.

First, we want to work out the difference between the old and new price: 92 - 55 = 37p. In consequence, with every bottle sold, I take 37p less than if I had kept the price higher. So the total shortfall in money is:

150 x 37 = 150 x 30 + 150 x 7 = 4500 + 1050 = **5550p or £55.50.**

We could also multiply 150 and 37 using the column method:

$$
\begin{array}{r}
1\overset{1}{5}0 \\
\times\ 37 \\
\hline
1050 \\
+4500 \\
\hline
5550
\end{array}
$$

Don't forget
to add this
extra zero
here
when
multiplying
by a two-digit
number!

Answer: 5550p or £55.50

10. What are the missing prime numbers?

41, 43, ?, ?, 59

We know both the missing numbers are between 43 and 59, so we need to check at most 16 numbers. First we know all prime numbers are odd (except 2) so we can immediately exclude half of the 16 numbers. Of the remaining 8, we can easily exclude the multiples of 5 — that is, those numbers that end in 5 or 0 — which leaves only 47, 49, 51, 53, 57.

We can also exclude $49 = 7^2$ if we know our square numbers. Identifying the last two numbers to exclude can be tricky.

One handy rule here is the fact that any number whose individual digits add up to a multiple of 3 are, themselves, a multiple of 3. For instance, if we take 123, we can see that $1+2+3 = 6$, which is itself a multiple of 3 – and, therefore, 123 is a multiple of 3.

Using this trick, we can see that both 51 (5+1 = 6) and 57 (5+7 = 12) are multiples of 3, thereby allowing us to eliminate both of these digits. Thus the only numbers left are **47 and 53.**

Usually it's best to find primes by excluding non-primes rather than identifying one by trying every number to see if it is a divisor. Even though this explanation was long, this was to provide you with some methodologies to help you solve these problems more quickly in the future!

Answer: 47 and 53

11. a. Write down the value of these Roman numerals:

- $\underline{V}$
- $\underline{L}$

b. What year is written in Roman numerals as MMXIV?

(a)

First we need to know our Roman numerals, I, V, X, L, C, D and M represent 1, 5, 10, 50, 100, 500, 1000, respectively.

Accordingly, then, **V is 5** and **L is 50.**

Answer: V is 5, L is 50

(b)

The year is MM = 2000, X = 10 and IV = 4, so adding these numbers we get:

2000 + 10 + 4 = **2014**.

When it comes to Roman numerals, you need to remember that they are 'paired'. By this I mean that we represent each digit of a number using at most two different types of letters. In the units column we can make the numbers 1 to 9 with only I and V. We can represent the tens column (the numbers 10, 20, ..., 90) with only the letters X and L. So if you see a long sequence of roman numbers, break it into pairs of I, V, and X, L, and C, D etc. then add up these numbers to find the full number.

Answer: <u>2014</u>

12. Write 90 as a product of its prime factors.

We can do this sequentially by dividing by primes from small to large.

90 = 2 x 45 = 2 x 3 x 15 = 2 x 3 x 3 x 5. So 90 = **2 x 3^2 x 5**.

Another way of visualising this is with the ladder method. You take the number in question, and divide it by the smallest prime number you can – so that 90 becomes 45 when divided by 2 – and then we move up to the next biggest prime number. In this case, 45 can be divided by 3 to give us 15; and then 15 can also be divided by 3 to give us 5.

5 is not divisible by 3. But it *can* be divided by the next largest prime number – 5 – once.

To write 90 as a product of its prime factors, we just multiply all the numbers on the left-hand side of the ladder: 2 x 3 x 3 x 5. So 90 = **2 x 3^2 x 5**.

Answer: <u>2 x 3^2 x 5</u>

13. In the sequence 3, 4, 6, 10, 18, ... what is the first three digit number that appears?

As with most sequences, we start by looking at the difference in terms. First we add 1, then 2, then 4, 8, etc. — in other words, we are doubling the difference each time. So we will need to add 16, 32, 64, and so forth. We can then add these to 18, getting first 34, then 66, and finally 130.

So the answer is **130.**

Answer: 130

14. Which name best describes the below shape?

- **Prism**
- **Pyramid**
- **Heptadecagon**

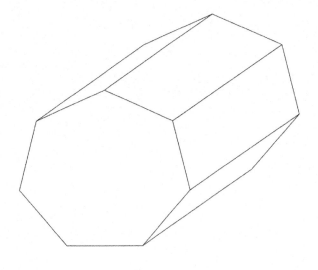

The correct answer is **prism**.

A prism is a 3D shape with two faces (called bases) that are congruent and parallel. These two bases can then be joined by rectangles (or more generally, parallelograms).

What we are looking at is definitely not a pyramid, as there are no triangles.

Finally, a heptadecagon is a 17 sided polygon and is not a 3D shape, and thus it is not the correct answer. You wouldn't be required to know this specific information about heptadecagons — rather, the examiner is expecting us to deduce the correct answer based on our understanding of what a prism is!

Answer: Prism

15. a. Label North, East, South, and West on the compass below.

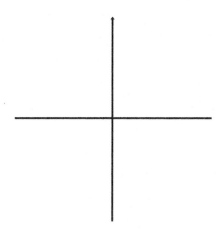

b. If I am facing East, and turn 125 degrees clockwise 3 times, then a further 75 degrees, which direction am I facing?

(a)

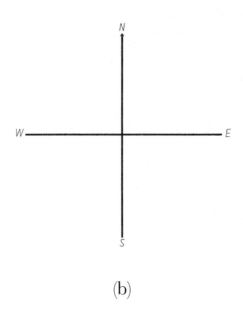

(b)

First we work out how far I turned in total, which is 125 x 3 + 75 = 375 +75 = 450. We notice this is more than one full turn so we can break it into two turns: 450 = 360 + 90.

The first 360 will get me back to turning east, then an additional 90 will leave me facing south.

Answer: South

16. Consider the diagram below. Lines MN and PQ are parallel.

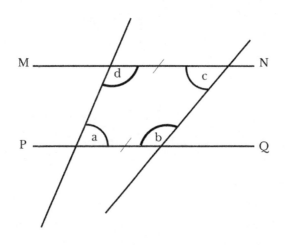

a. If a = 70, what is d?

b. Now we change b and c to right angles (as can be seen in the diagram below). If a = 70, what is d?

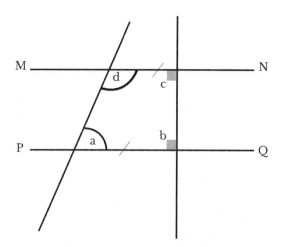

c. Given the last two examples, if I have a new line crossing MN and PQ, what must be the sum of angles x and y?

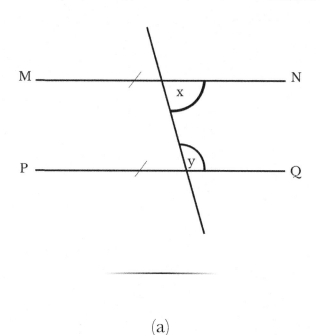

(a)

We know the interior angles of a quadrilateral must add up to 360. If you were not aware of this or don't believe me, consider the following diagram, where a quadrilateral is formed from two triangles. The sum of the interior angles of a triangle is 180, so the sum of all the angles in both must be 360. Any quadrilateral you draw can be divided this way.

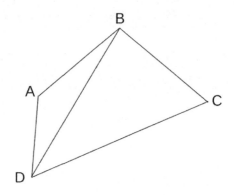

Given this, we must have d = 360 - a - b - c = **110**.

Answer: 110

(b)

For the second part we could equally calculate 360 - a - 90 - 90, but we could also simply note that we haven't done anything which would change d, so d must be the same and thus d = **110**.

Answer: 110

(c)

For the final part, we can note that we can think about adding a perpendicular line cutting MN and PQ like so, then we must have 90 + 90 + x + y =360 so x+y = **180**.

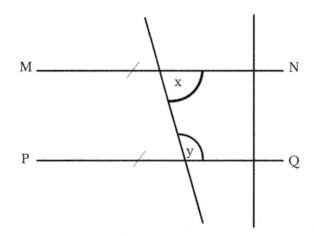

This has shown us that whenever we have two parallel lines cut by a straight line as shown above, the angles x and y must sum to 180.

Answer: <u>180</u>

17. Simplify the following ratios:

a) 42 : 6

b) 15 : 35

c) 6 : 22

(a)

When simplifying ratios we are looking to eliminate common factors from both sides. We could do this systematically by dividing by primes from smallest upwards. Alternatively, we might notice that 6 x 7 = 42, and so we can divide both sides by 6, getting **7:1**.

Answer: <u>7:1</u>

(b)

We notice that both digits are both multiples of 5, and so dividing both sides by 5 we have **3:7**. These figures both share no factors (we can say they are coprime), and thus the ratio cannot be simplified further — in fact they are both primes, which are always coprime.

Answer: <u>3:7</u>

(c)

We can divide by 2, giving us **3:11**. Since these are both primes, we can simplify no further.

Answer: <u>3:11</u>

18. In Oslo the temperature is -15C and in Berlin it is 11C. How much warmer is it in Berlin than in Oslo?

All this question requires is that we are comfortable with negative numbers. We can first count to 0, then to 11 to ensure no mistakes. -15 is 15 less than 0, then we need to add on an additional 11, giving 15 + 11 = 26C

Answer: <u>26C</u>

19. Two numbers, A and B, have two distinct prime factors each, neither of which they have in common. Their difference is 1. They are both less than 22. A is bigger than B. What is B?

Though this problem might seem tough as there are many possibilities, we can quickly reduce how many numbers we need to check. If the numbers are less than 22, then so are their factors, and the primes below 22 are 2, 3, 5, 7, 11, 13, 17, 19.

If we need two prime factors for both numbers which are less than 22, then we can immediately eliminate 11, 13, 17, 19 as potential prime factors, since the smallest other prime factor can be 2, and double any of these numbers is equal or over 22.

This leaves only 2, 3, 5 and 7, which can be combined in 3 different ways:

A = 5 x 7 = 12, B = 2 x 3 = 6

A = 3 x 7 = 21, B = 2 x 5 = 10

A = 5 x 3 = 15, B = 2 x 7 = 14

So A =15 and B = 14

You can also just try testing finding all numbers below 22 which have only two prime factors. If we write out the numbers below 22 which are not prime, this gives 1, 4, 6, 8, 9, 10, 12, 14, 15, 16, 18, 20, 21. Then we only need to check the pairs of consecutive numbers, 8,9 and 9,10, and 14,15 and 15,16 and 20,21. There are only 5 to check and we can eliminate invalid ones quite quickly.

Answer: A =15 and B = 14

20. If I am 90 years, 80 months, 70 weeks and 60 days old today, how many complete years have I lived?

The first thing to notice is that we have to convert the months, weeks and days into years.

There are 12 months in a year so 80 months is 80 ÷ 12 years which is 6 remainder 8. So we have an additional 6 years and we need to keep track of those 8 extra months. We'll add up all our remainders at the end.

There are 52 weeks in a year, so 70 ÷ 52 is 1 remainder 18, so that gives another 1 year.

There are 365 days in a year, so we have 0 additional years with 60 days remaining.

This gives us a total of 7 additional years to the 90 given in the question, but we still have a remainder for each value we need to also add on. There are a couple of ways to do this.

We could note that the 8 months take us from January to August, so we have September, October, November and December still to get through before another additional year to count. This time period consists of 30 + 31 + 30 + 31 = 122 days. We still have 18 weeks and 60 days to add on. In total this consists of 18 x 7 + 60 = 186 days. As this is greater than 122, this brings my total age to 90 + 7 + 1 years and 186 - 122 days, or 98 years and 64 days.

So the answer is **98 years**.

Answer: <u>98 years</u>

Exam Paper Four

60 Minutes | 20 Questions

Practice Paper Four

1. In each of the following, find "?"

   a) 23 x 32 = ?

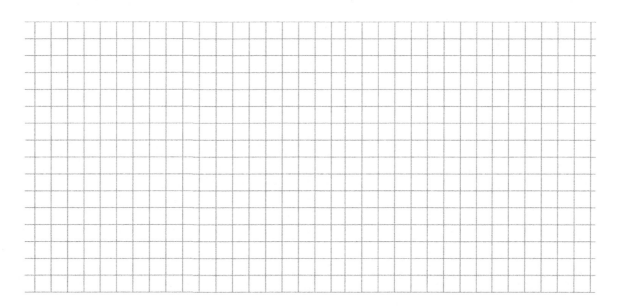

                                        Answer:_____

b) 14941 + 94149 = ?

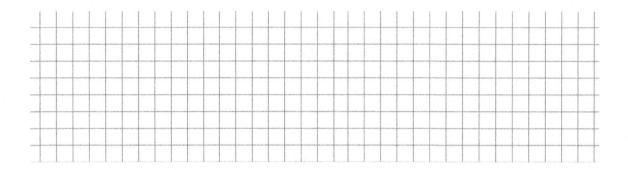

Answer:_____

c) 303 ÷ 3 = ?

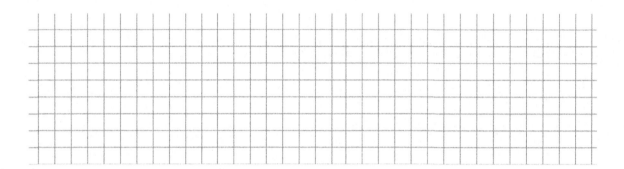

Answer:_____

d) 171 - 717 = ?

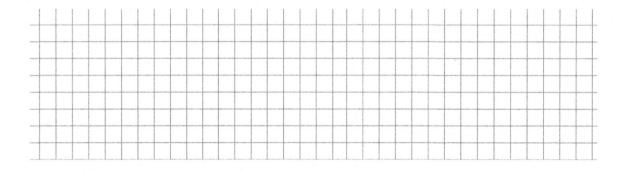

Answer:_____

2. Using the numbers below, fill in the dotted lines.

81, 29, 51, 66, 36, 14, 102, 123

a) A square number ....

b) An even number which is a multiple of 18 ....

c) A multiple of 7 which is also a factor of 56 ....

d) A prime number ....

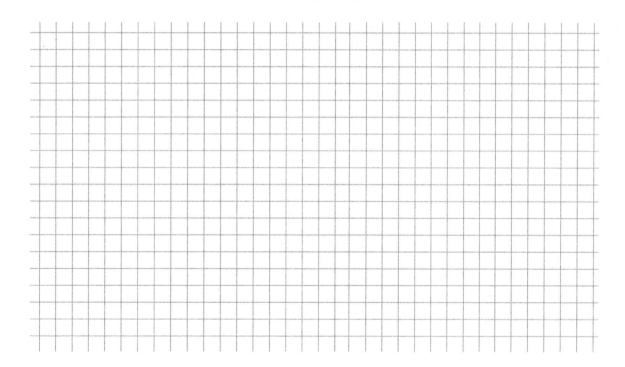

3. Write down the number forty thousand and thirteen in digits.

Answer:_____

4. Write down the following tally in digits:

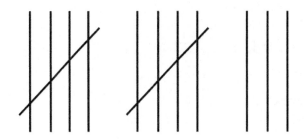

Answer:_____

5. Do the three coordinates A = (-4,3), B = (-2,2) and C = (2, 0) form a triangle?

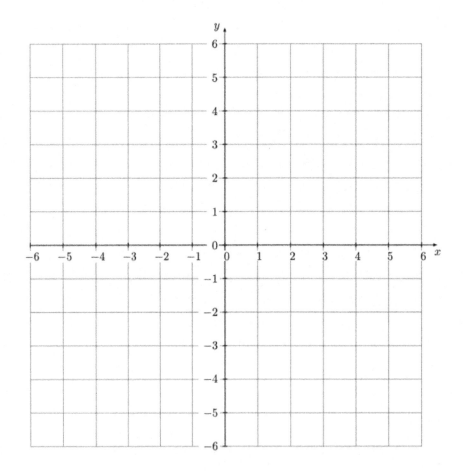

Circle the correct answer: Yes | No

6. How many lines of symmetry does a regular heptagon (shown below) have?

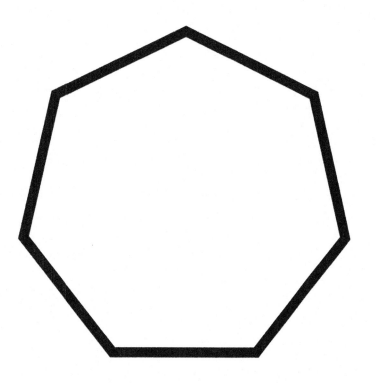

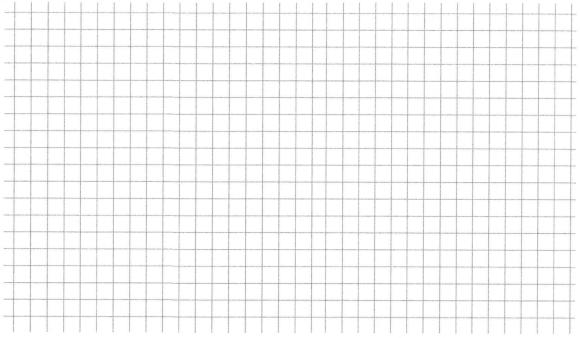

Answer:_____

7. There are 5 players in a table tennis tournament. If every player must play every other player twice, how many matches will there be?

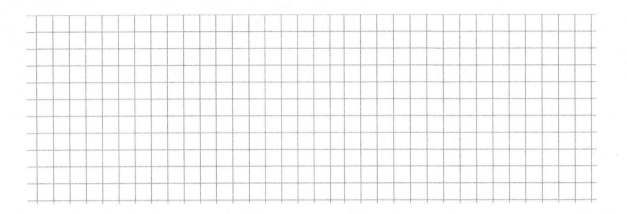

Answer:_____

8. The diagram consists of points representing towns connected by roads. Each road is labeled with the time it takes to travel from one end to the other in minutes.

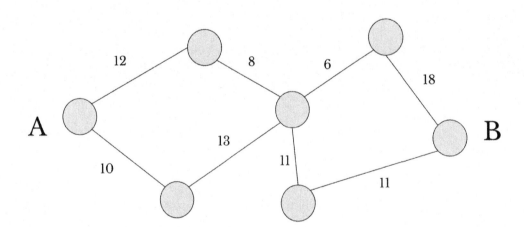

a. What is the shortest amount of time I can take to travel from point A to point B?

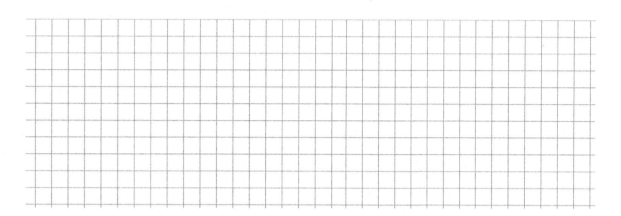

Answer:_____

b. What is the longest time I could take?

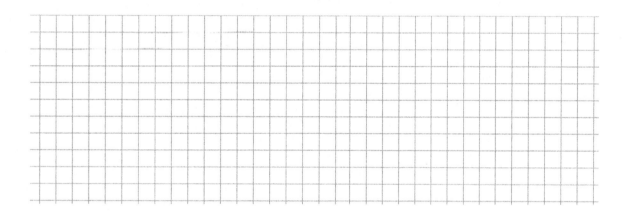

Answer:_____

c. Draw on the diagram a new road between two towns, which takes 21 minutes to travel down but will change what the quickest path is.

9. Write out the coordinates of the triangle on the diagram below, after it has been translated 4 squares to the right and 3 down.

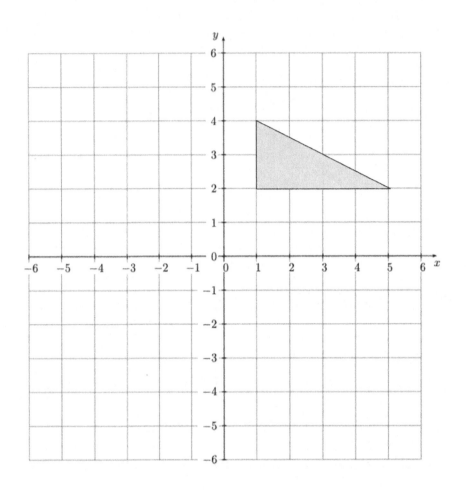

Answer:_____

10. A train leaves Farringdon at 11:56 and arrives in Reading at 13:47. How long was the journey?

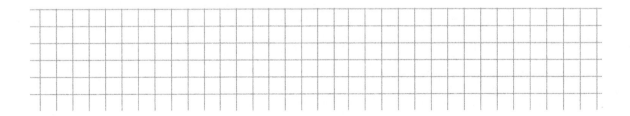

Answer:_____

11. 3 boxes of equal size are stacked as shown below.

The total volume of the stack below is 81cm³. Work out the height of the stack.

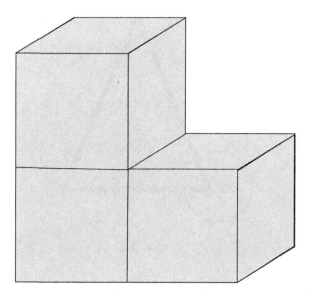

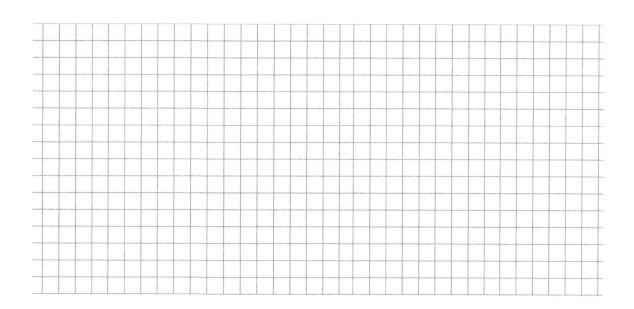

Answer:_____

12. Given the triangle below is isosceles, find the angle labelled A.

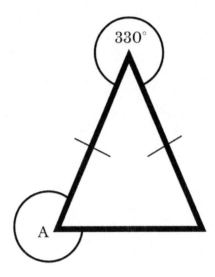

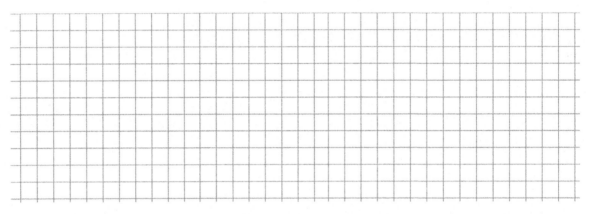

Answer:_____

13. What is 426 minutes in hours and minutes?

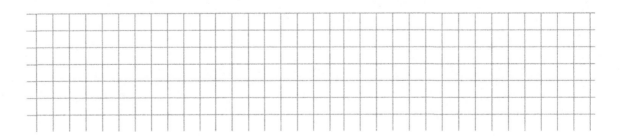

Answer:_____

14. Izzy notices that the digits of 482 add up to 14. She looks at some other numbers then announces that she has found a 3 digit number where the product of its digits is 102. Explain why Izzy must be wrong.

Answer:

_____

_____

_____

15. Below, the net of a cuboid is drawn. Write B next to the side which will be in contact with the side label A.

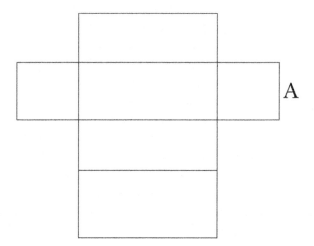

16. In my classroom I sit at a table of six people with my class-mates Anne, Beth, Clara, Diane and Elisa. Anne sits between Beth and Clara. Beth and Clara also make an equilateral triangle shape with me. Beth is on Diane's right. Where are we all seated?

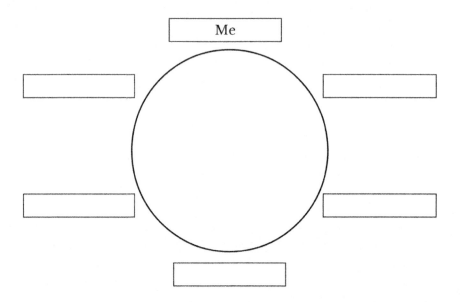

17. In twelve years time, Martin will be twice as old as he is now. How old is Martin?

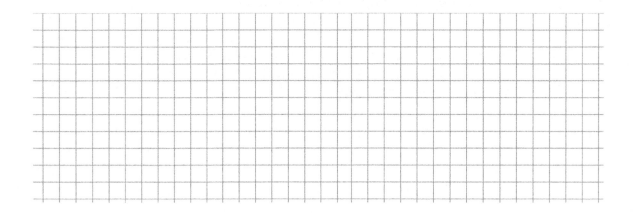

Answer:_____

18. The salaries of 5 people are given in the table below:

Person	Salary
Jim	$42,500
Pam	$21,000
Michael	$68,000
Stanley	$38,000
Meredith	$42,000

a. What is the mean salary of the office?

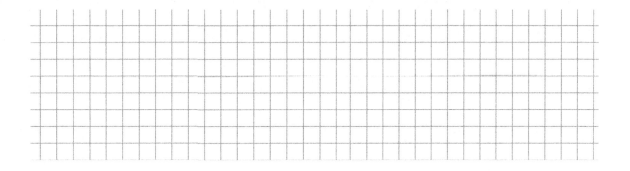

Answer:_____

b. Due to budget cuts, everyone in the office must take a salary reduction of 20%. What is the new average salary?

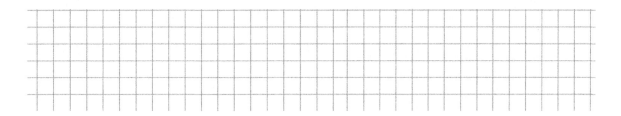

Answer:_____

19. There are *m* cows and *n* spiders in a shed, plus the farmer's son Tim. No animal or person is missing a leg.

    a. Write down an algebraic expression for the number of legs in the shed.

                                Answer:_____

    b. If the total number of legs in the shed is 42, write down an equation involving *m* and *n*, simplified as much as possible.

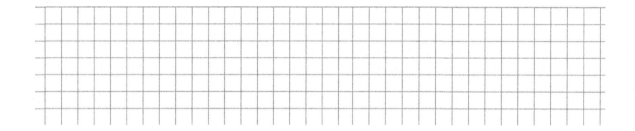

                                Answer:_____

20. Three runners are running a 100m race.

Mike runs the first half at 10 m/s and the second half at 8 m/s

Phil runs the first third at 11 m/s, the second third at 10 m/s and the final third at 9 m/s

Jacob will run the first quarter at 12 m/s the second quarter at 11 m/s, the third quarter at 10 m/s and the final quarter at 9 m/s

Who will win the race?

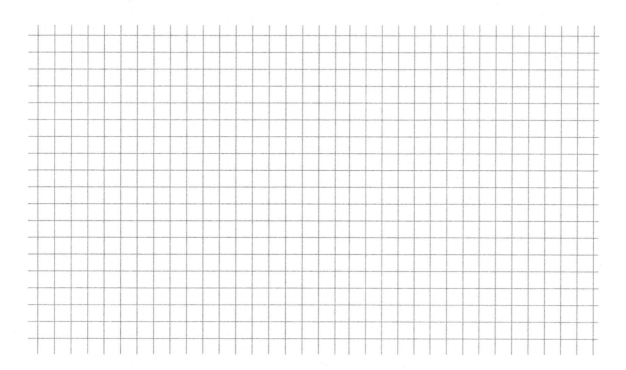

Answer:_____

Answers and Guidance

1. In each of the following, find "?"

a) 23 x 32 = ?

b) 14941 + 94149 = ?

c) 303 ÷ 3 = ?

d) 171 - 717 = ?

Each of a, b and c only require relatively straightforward calculation, so we will just write the answers.

(a)

Answer: 736

(b)

Answer: 109090

(c)

Answer: 101

(d)

For (d) we are clearly going to end up with a negative number. One method is to count backwards first to 0, then further to the answer. Noting that 717 - 171 = 546. That is, 171 - 717 = 171 - 171 - 546 = 0 - 546 = **-546**.

However, a quicker way to deal with subtractions involving negatives is as follows:

171 - 717 = -1 x (717 - 171) = -1 x (546) = -546

Answer: -546

2. Using the numbers below, fill in the dotted lines.

81, 29, 51, 66, 36, 14, 102, 123

a. A square number ....

b. An even number which is a multiple of 18 ....

c. A multiple of 7 which is also a factor of 56 ....

d. A prime number ....

(a)

The first number in the list is **81** = 9x9.

Answer: 81

(b)

We note that as 2 is a factor of 18, every multiple of 18 is even, so we just need to find a multiple of 18 in this list. 2 x 18 = **36**, which is in the list, and is therefore the correct answer.

Answer: 36

(c)

56 ÷ 7 = 8, so the possible factors of 56 which are multiples of 7 are

7, 7 x 2, 7 x 2 x 2, 7 x 2 x 2 x 2. These are 7, 14, 28, 56. The only one in the list is **14**.

Alternatively, a student could simply notice that 14 is the only number in the list that is a multiple of 7 at all!

Answer: 14

(d)

All the numbers in the list are even except 29, 81, 51, 123. All of these are multiples of 3 (check the sums of the digits) except 29, so **29** must be the prime number.

Answer: 29

3. Write down the number forty thousand and thirteen in digits.

Forty thousand is 40,000; then we just need to add 13, so the answer is **40,013**.

Answer: 40,013

4. Write down the following tally in digits:

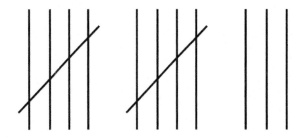

With tally marks we just need to remember that:

$$\cancel{||||} = 5$$

… and that a single line is 1. In light of this, we can count 2 groups of 5 plus 3. So, we have: 2 x 5 + 3 = **13**

Answer: 13

5. Do the three coordinates A = (-4,3), B = (-2,2) and C = (2, 0) form a triangle?

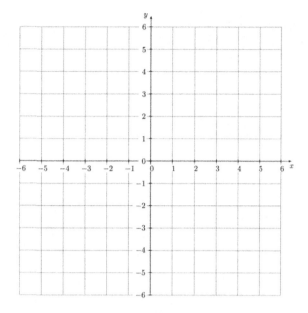

In general any three points will form a triangle so long as they do not all lie on a straight line — and if they *do* all lie on a straight line, we say they are collinear. If we draw all these points on a coordinate axis we see they do in fact all lie on a line, **so they don't form a triangle.**

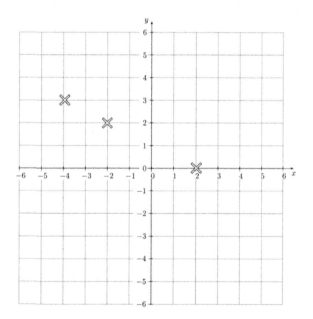

Answer: No

6. How many lines of symmetry does a regular heptagon (shown below) have?

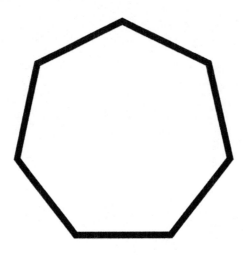

We can first note there is at least one line of symmetry directly down the middle. Then as the shape is regular, we can rotate it 7 times and get exactly the same shape, so there must be exactly **7 lines of symmetry**. In general a regular polygon with *n* sides will have *n* lines of symmetry.

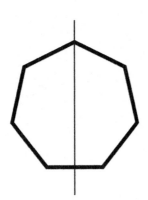
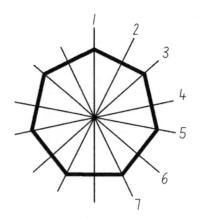

Answer: 7

7. There are 5 players in a table tennis tournament. If every player must play every other player twice, how many matches will there be?

First we can work out how many matches there will be if every competitor plays each other once, then double that number. One nice way to visualise the problem is to draw each player as a point, and mark a game between them with a line. We worked out in a previous exam that the number of lines (matches) here was 5 x 4 / 2 = 10. So now we just need to double this number and so the answer is **20**.

If you don't think you would've visualised the problem in this way, you can also label the players A, B, C, D, E, and write out all the pairs we can choose from these 5: AB, BC, CD etc. Then we have 5 options for the first letter of the pair, and 5 for the second, so this gives us 5 x 5 =25 possible pairs, but we must then subtract 5 pairs (AA, BB, CC, DD, EE) as a person cannot play themselves.

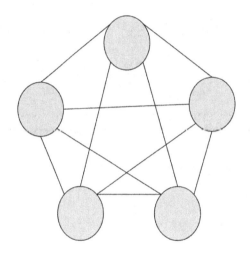

Answer: 20

8. The diagram consists of points representing towns connected by roads. Each road is labeled with the time it takes to travel from one end to the other in minutes.

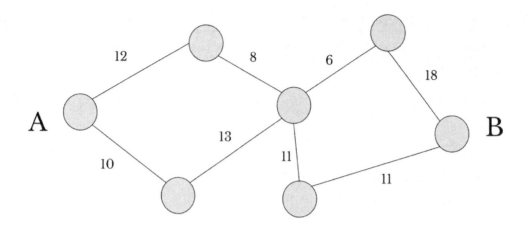

a. What is the shortest amount of time I can take to travel from point A to point B?

b. What is the longest time I could take?

c. Draw on the diagram a new road between two towns, which takes 21 minutes to travel down but will change what the quickest path is.

(a)

I'm going to add a label to one of the other towns in the diagram, and we will call X.

Notice that whatever path I take from A to B, I must pass through X. This allows us to split the problem into two slightly smaller problems.

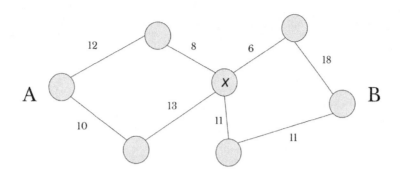

If we take the upper path from A to X, this takes 12+8=20 minutes, and if we take the lower path this takes 10 +13 = 23 minutes. If we take the lower path from X to B this takes 22 minutes. And if we take the upper path from X to B this takes 24 minutes. So the shortest path consists of the upper path from A to X and the lower path from X to B, taking 20 + 22 = **42 minutes**.

Answer: 42 Minutes

(b)

The longest path instead consists of the lower path from A to X and the upper path from X to B, which amounts to 23 + 24 = **47 minutes.**

Answer: 47 Minutes

(c)

The new road has also been added on the diagram below, which allows a direct line from A to B.

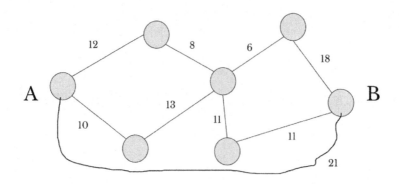

9. Write out the coordinates of the triangle on the diagram below, after it has been translated 4 squares to the right and 3 down.

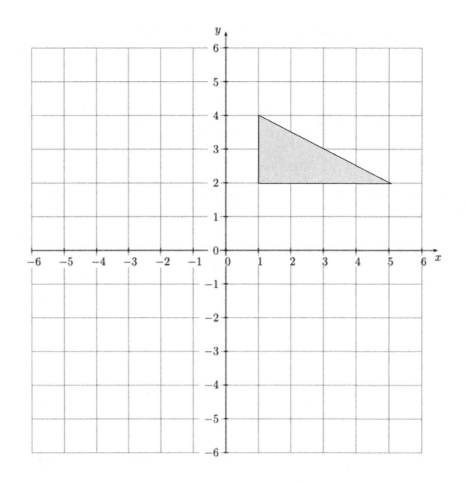

First we write out the coordinates of the triangle, which are (1,4), (5,2) and (1,2). To translate the shape 4 squares to the right is to add 4 to each of these x coordinates (if we were going left we would subtract) and subtract 3 from each of the y coordinates (as we are going down).

Thus the final coordinates are **(5,1), (9,-1) and (5,-1)**.

Answer: <u>(5,1), (9,-1) and (5,-1)</u>

10. A train leaves Farringdon at 11:56 and arrives in Reading at 13:47. How long was the journey?

It's 4 minutes until 12:00, then another 47 until 12:47, so 51 minutes in total. Then it's another hour until 13:47; so the total is **1 hour 51 minutes**.

Answer: <u>1 hour and 51 minutes</u>

11. 3 boxes of equal size are stacked as shown below.

The total volume of the stack below is 81cm³. Work out the height of the stack.

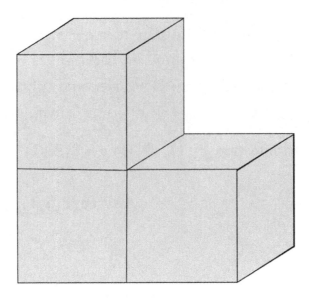

The plan will be to find the side length of one of the cubes, then to double this value. The volume of a single cube is $81 \div 3 = 27\text{cm}^3$.

The cube numbers below 100 are 1, 8, 27 and 64. These are useful to know as if a cube has side length X, then its volume will be X^3. For example, if a cube has side length 2cm, then its volume is 8cm^3. So if each cube has volume 27cm^3, we can therefore infer that they must each have side length 3cm.

So we now have $3^3 = 27$, so the side length of each cube is 3. Thus the height of the stack is twice the length of a single cube which is 3 x 2 = **6cm**.

Answer: <u>6cm</u>

12. Given the triangle below is isosceles, find the angle labelled A.

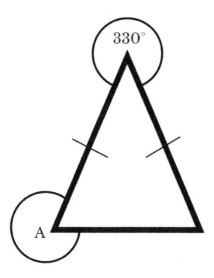

We're going to label a few more angles for reference

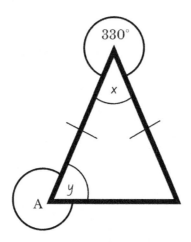

We can work out x as follows: x = 360 - 330 = 30. And y+ y + 30 = 180 as the triangle is isosceles and angles in a triangle sum to 180. As such, we know that y = 75. Therefore, A = 360 - 75 = **285**.

Answer: 285

13. What is 426 minutes in hours and minutes?

We need to divide 426 by 60 and find the remainder. Note 60 x 7 = 420 so 420 / 60 = 7 with remainder 6; so the answer is **7 hours and 6 minutes**.

Answer: 7 hours and 6 minutes

14. Izzy notices that the digits of 482 add up to 14. She looks at some other numbers then announces that she has found a 3 digit number where the product of its digits is 102. Explain why Izzy must be wrong.

We're going to look at the factors of 102. This number is even so we divide it by 2 and get 51. The sum of the digits of 51 is 6 which is a multiple of 3, so 3 must also be a factor of 51. Dividing 51 by 3 we get 17 which is prime, so we can write: 102 = 2 x 3 x 17 which is the prime factorisation of 102.

Now clearly Izzy must be wrong. 17 is a prime factor of 102. It cannot be one of the three digits that make up Izzy's number (because 17 is a two-digit number) and no amount of single digit numbers can be multiplied together to give a multiple of 17, since 17 is prime. **So in essence: Izzy must be wrong, as 102 has a prime factor that is greater than 10.**

. . .

15. Below, the net of a cuboid is drawn. Write B next to the side which will be in contact with the side label A.

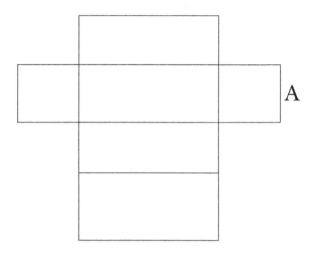

This is somewhat tricky to explain, as it tests your visualisation skills. If you are not convinced, cut out the net of a cuboid and practice constructing it.

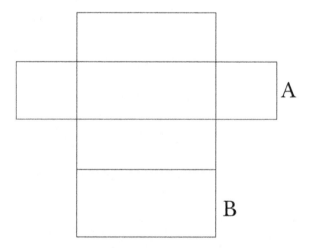

16. In my classroom I sit at a table of six people with my class-mates Anne, Beth, Clara, Diane and Elisa. Anne sits between Beth and Clara. Beth and Clara also make an equilateral triangle shape with me. Beth is on Diane's right. Where are we all seated?

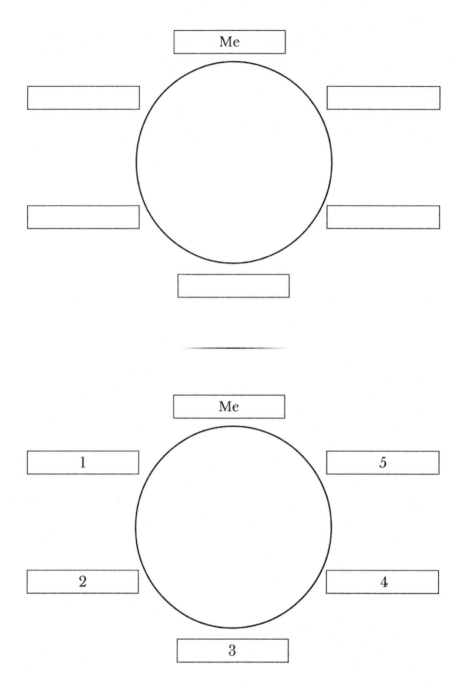

To make things easier to understand, we will denote the blank spaces by numbers 1 to 5 and refer to them while explaining the answer.

We know that Anne is between Beth and Clara, so she cannot be seated in 1 or 5, or I would be one of her neighbours. Also, Beth and Clara form an equilateral triangle with me, so they must be seated in numbers 2 and 4, which makes Anne's seat number 3. This means that Diane and Elisa are in numbers 1 and 5.

Finally, Beth is on Diane's right. If Diane was seated in number 5, I would be on her right, so her seat must be 1. Hence, Beth's is 2, Clara's is 4 and Elisa's is 5. You can see this arrangement in the following picture:

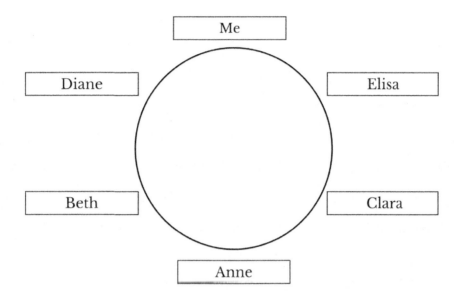

17. In twelve years time, Martin will be twice as old as he is now. How old is Martin?

This is a problem which some basic algebra can make a lot clearer. Let's use "X" to connote Martin's age. We know that x + 12 = 2x. Making x the subject of this equation by subtracting x from both sides, we have 12 = x; so Martin is **12**.

Answer: <u>12</u>

18. The salaries of 5 people are given in the table below:

Person	Salary
Jim	$42,500
Pam	$21,000
Michael	$68,000
Stanley	$38,000
Meredith	$42,000

a. What is the mean salary of the office?

b. Due to budget cuts, everyone in the office must take a salary reduction of 20%. What is the new average salary?

(a)

First we sum the 5 numbers in the table, the total is 211500. We then need to divide this by 5. This is the same as doubling, then dividing by 10. Double 211500 = 423000. We then divide this by 10, and our answer is **$42,300**.

Answer: $42,300

(b)

To calculate the new mean after salary reductions, we could take 20% off every number, sum and divide. Alternatively, we could see that this is the same as taking 20% off the sum we just calculated. We could also notice that 20% is the same as ⅕ — which is a figure we just calculated, as ⅕ is also the previous mean. So we need 211500 - 42300 = 169200.

We then need to divide this by 5, which gives us **$33,840**, the new mean salary.

Answer: $33,840

19. There are _m_ cows and _n_ spiders in a shed, plus the farmer's son Tim. No animal or person is missing a leg.

> **a. Write down an algebraic expression for the number of legs in the shed.**

> **b. If the total number of legs in the shed is 42, write down an equation involving _m_ and _n_, simplified as much as possible.**

(a)

We know people have two legs, cows have 4 and spiders have 8, so the number of legs in the shed is 2 x 1 + 4 x _m_ + 8 x _n_ = **2 + 4m + 8n**

Answer: 2 + 4m + 8n

(b)

If there are 42 legs in total we can write $2 + 4m + 8n = 42$, which we can simplify by dividing both sides by 2 to get $1 + 2m + 4n = 21$, we can simplify this further by subtracting 1 from both sides to get $2m + 4n = 20$. This last equation can again be simplified by dividing by 2, giving $m + 2n = 10$.

Answer: _m_ + 2n = 10

20. Three runners are running a 100m race.

Mike runs the first half at 10 m/s and the second half at 8 m/s

Phil runs the first third at 11 m/s, the second third at 10 m/s and the final third at 9 m/s

Jacob will run the first quarter at 12 m/s the second quarter at 11 m/s, the third quarter at 10 m/s and the final quarter at 9 m/s

Who will win the race?

In order to figure out who won the race, we could calculate everyone's times to see which is smallest, or we could take a slightly more clever approach…

Notice at no point in time is Mike moving faster than Phil: they are either going the same speed, or Mike is slower. By the same token, at no point are Mike or Phil moving faster than Jacob; so Jacob is always moving as fast or faster than the other two. Hence, Jacob must win the race.

Answer: Jacob

Exam Paper Five

60 Minutes | 20 Questions

Practice Paper Five

1. What is the largest even 6 digit number which can be made using the numbers 1, 3, 4, 5, 6, 7?

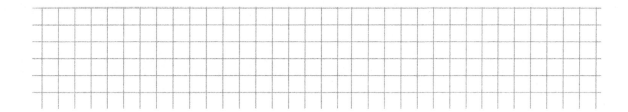

Answer:_____

2. I earn \$42,000/year as a salary, but give away 2% to charity. How much do I have left after this?

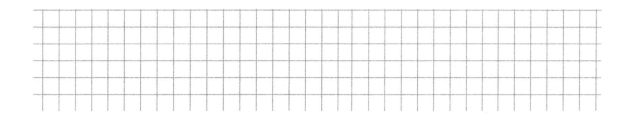

Answer:_____

3. Circle two numbers with a difference of 5

-3, -2, -1, 0 , 1, 2, 3

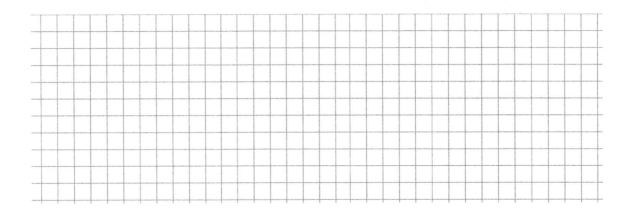

4. I have a deck of cards numbered 1 - 52 inclusive, with different shapes on each card. On every multiple of 6 there is a circle, and on every card which is a factor of 90 there is a square. If I draw a random card from somewhere in the deck, what is the probability that the card has both a circle and a square on it?

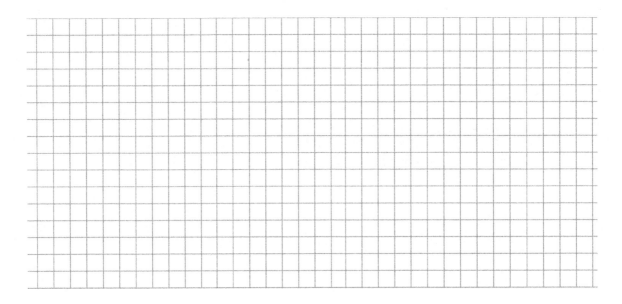

Answer:_____

5. a. What is the cube root of 1,000?

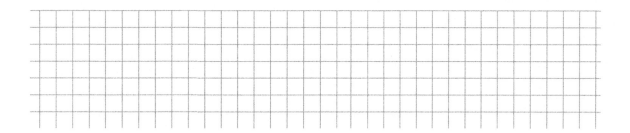

Answer:_____

b. What is the cube root of 1,000,000?

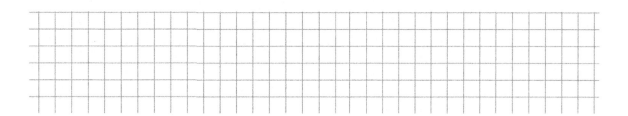

Answer:_____

6. I have two whole numbers *a* and *b*. I know that *a* is 170 less than *b* and also that:

a + b = 500

Find *b*

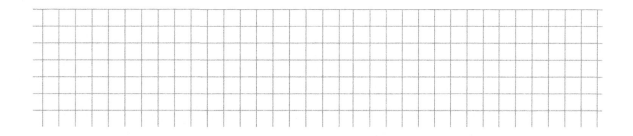

Answer:_____

7. Chris is 3 years older than Joseph. The sum of their ages is 79. What is Joseph's age?

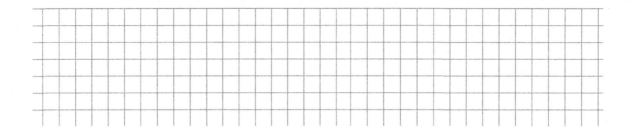

Answer:_____

8. The diagram below shows a pictogram with information about the number of people in 3 working groups in an office. Each smiley face represents 4 people. How many more people are in Group 3 than Group 1?

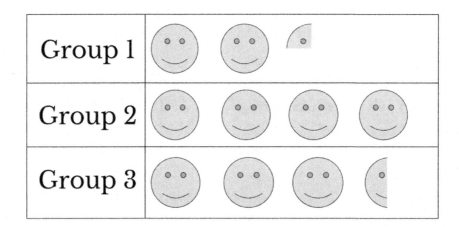

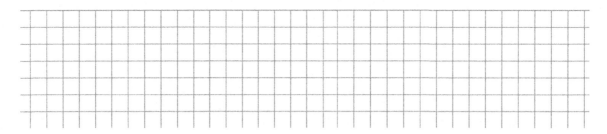

Answer:_____

9. The shape below is 4cm tall and 3cm wide. What is its perimeter?

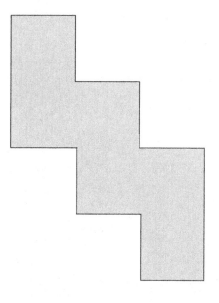

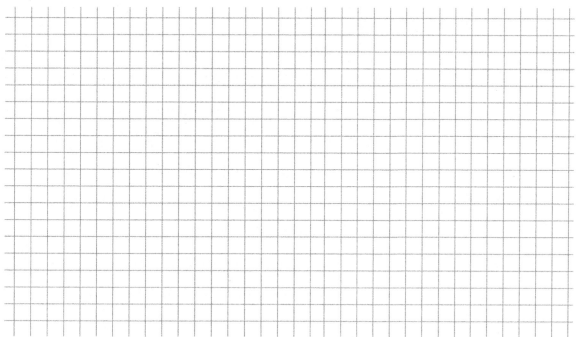

Answer:_____

10. If I roll a fair dice 42 times, how many times should I expect to get a 4?

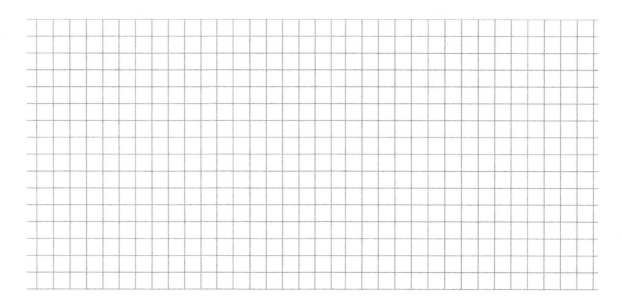

Answer:_____

11. Work out 43 - 16/2 x 3

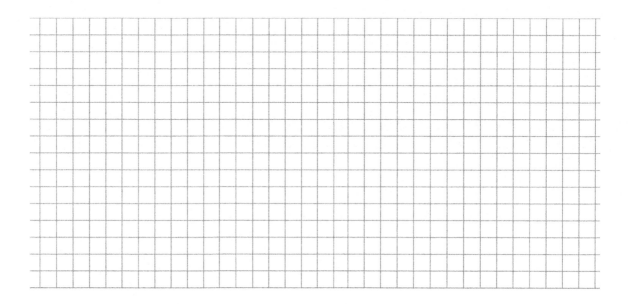

Answer:_____

12. We define a new mathematical operation by (|) where x (|) y means 'x-1 times y plus 3', so:

4 (|) 2 = (4-1) x 2 + 3 = 9

a) What is 12 (|) 4?

Answer:_____

b) What b is such that 8 (|) b = 52?

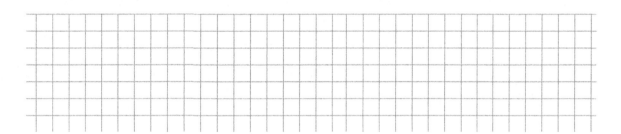

Answer:_____

c) Find c if (c+1) (|) c = 67

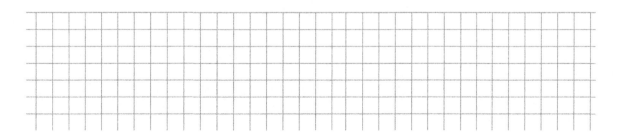

Answer:_____

13. Here is a list of ingredients to make 12 gluten-free brownies:

- **300g cornflour**
- **150g sugar**
- **100g butter**
- **3 eggs**
- **200g chocolate**

How many eggs and how much chocolate do I need to make 8 brownies? Leave your answers rounded to the nearest whole number.

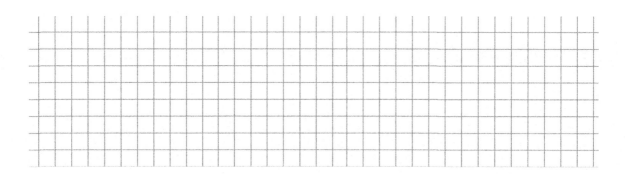

Answer:_____

14. How many <u>squares</u> are there altogether in the below diagram?

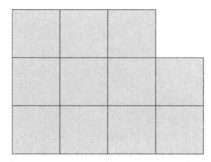

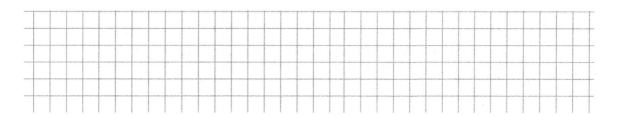

Answer:_____

15. a. What is the coordinate of the point (-2, 1) when it is reflected in the y axis?

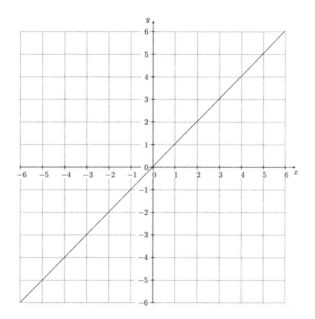

b. What about when the point (-2, 1) is reflected in the line y = x (which is drawn for you above)?

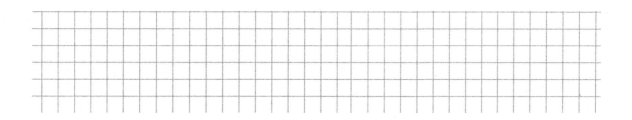

Answer:_____

16. The diagram below shows two parallel lines marked with arrows, being crossed by two other lines. The angles this figure forms are labelled.

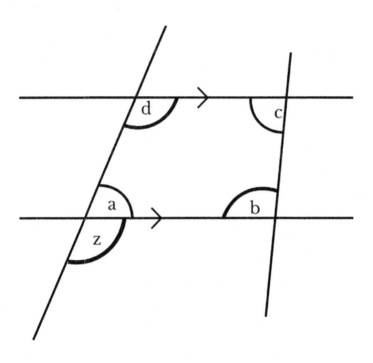

a. Given z = 120°, what is a?

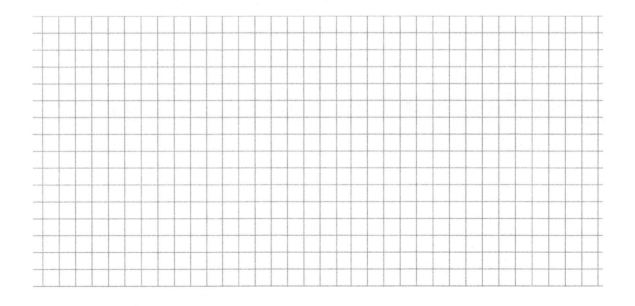

Answer:_____

b. Given b = 110°, c = 70°, what is d?

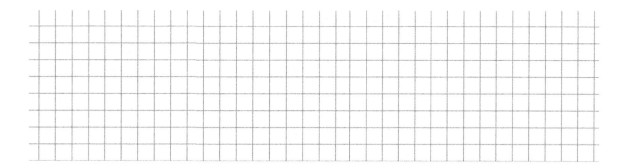

Answer:_____

c. Finally, look at the diagram below. If now z= 63, what is d?

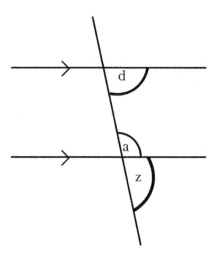

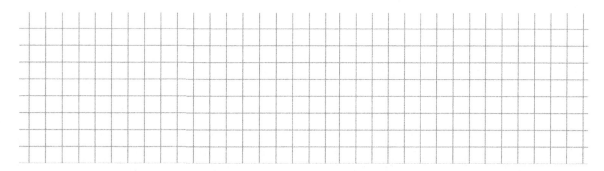

Answer:_____

17. X is a whole number which I do not know.

a. What is the mean of X+1 and X-1?

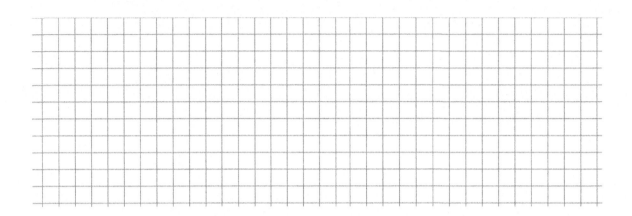

Answer:_____

b. What about X-1 and X+3?

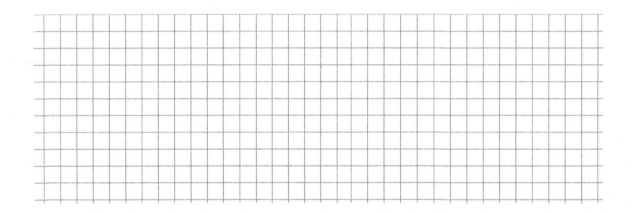

Answer:_____

18. Akmed replaces every letter of the alphabet with a number in a code. If R + A + T = 13 and T + R + A + P = 20, find the value of P.

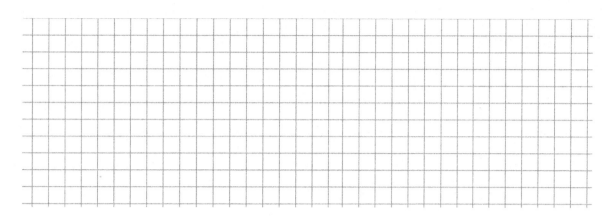

Answer:_____

19. At a pizza restaurant, the waiter tells me he has run out of 8 inch wide pizzas, so I can have two 4 inch wide pizzas for the same price. The area of a pizza is approximately 3.14 x r^2, where r is half the width. Will I get more pizza if I take the waiter's offer?

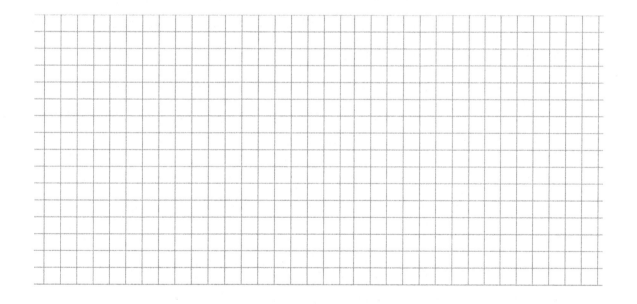

Circle the correct answer: Yes | No

20.

a. Write 36 as a product of its prime factors.

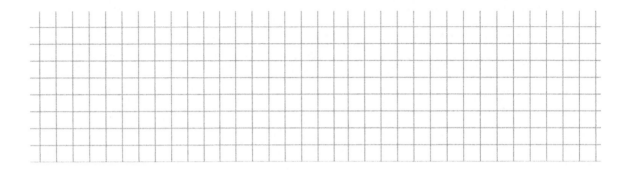

Answer:_____

b. I'm thinking of a number which has the prime factorisation
$2 \times 2 \times \underline{} \times 7 \times 11 \times \underline{}$

Given that my number is a square number, what are the prime factors in the blank spaces?

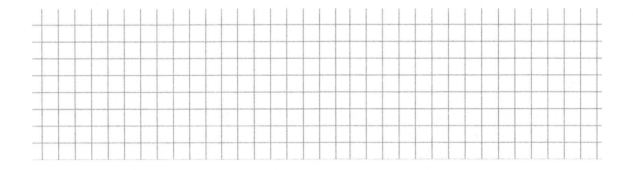

Answer:_____

c. Write the smallest square number which is even and also a multiple of 17.

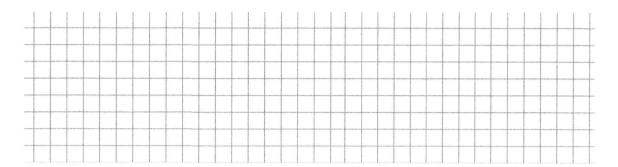

Answer:_____

Answers and Guidance

1. What is the largest even 6 digit number which can be made using the numbers 1, 3, 4, 5, 6, 7?

We need to use all the numbers given, and so we should start with 7 and descend.

The biggest number we could possibly make (odd or even) would be 765431, but this is odd, so we need to shuffle round 431 to get **765314**.

Answer: 765314

2. I earn $42,000/year as a salary, but give away 2% to charity. How much do I have left after this?

We either need to do 42,000/100 x 2 or 42,000/50 to find out how much I give away. Either way the answer is 840. Then 42000 - 840 = **41160**.

Another way to attack this is to do 42,000 x 0.98, which would tell you what 98% of 42,000 is. One way to crunch this would be to use the column method:

$$
\begin{array}{r}
4\,{}^{1}2000 \\
\times\ 0.98 \\
\hline
336000 \\
+3780000 \\
\hline
41160.00 \\
\hline
\end{array}
$$

The decimal point in 0.98 can cause some confusion when using the column method: where do we put the decimal point in the final answer?

Here's a trick. Look at the two numbers you are multiplying, and, for each, ask yourself: how many "jumps" in from the right-hand side does the decimal point appear.

In 42,000, there is no decimal point, so that is 0 "jumps" in from the right. In 0.98, the decimal point appears two "jumps" in from the right-hand side.

You then add these two sets of "jumps" together: 0 + 2 = 2.

We then go ahead and multiply the numbers, ignoring the decimal point for the time being. Then we look at the final figure, and place the decimal point 2 "jumps" in from the right -- that is, the total number of "jumps" present in the two numbers we are multiplying together.

Answer: 41160

3. Circle two numbers with a difference of 5.

-3, -2, -1, 0 , 1, 2, 3

There are multiple options here as we have 7 numbers in total. As they are all consecutive, there must be 2 pairs that are a distance of 5 apart. If you're having trouble spotting them, you can count backwards from 0 to 5. This gives you the pairs 0,5 then -1, 4 then **-2, 3** then **-3,2.** Either of these last two are acceptable answers.

Answer: -2, 3 or -3,2

4. I have a deck of cards numbered 1 - 52 inclusive, with different shapes on each card. On every multiple of 6 there is a circle, and on every card which is a factor of 90 there is a square. If I draw a random card from somewhere in the deck, what is the probability that the card has both a circle and a square on it?

We can list the factors of 90 with the prime factorisation:

90 = 9 x 10 = 3 x 3 x 2 x 5 = 6 x 3 x 5.

Using the ladder method, which can be seen on the righthand side of the page, we can visualise this process. We multiply all the numbers on the left-hand side of the ladder to get the prime factorisation.

From this we know that 6, 6 x 3, 6 x 5 and 6 x 3 x 5 are all factors of 90 which are also multiples of 6. That is 6, 18, 30 and 90.

We need numbers which are less than 52, so 6, 18 and 30. So three cards in all.

So now we need the probability of pulling one of these cards from the pack of 52 cards. This gives us the proportion 3/52 which cannot be further simplified, so our answer is 3/52.

Answer: 3/52

5. a. What is the cube root of 1,000?

b. What is the cube root of 1,000,000?

(a)

It is straightforward to see that $10^3 = 1000$, so the answer is **10**.

Answer: 10

(b)

The previous answer could inspire us to choose 100 as the next number to cube, and indeed 100 x 100 x 100 = 1,000,000. So the answer is **100**.

Answer: 100

6. I have two whole numbers *a* and *b*. I know that *a* is 170 less than *b* and also that:

$a + b = 500$

Find *b*.

We can write out the first piece of information as *b - a = 170*. Then we can make *a* the subject of this, to get *170 + a = b*. Then we can substitute this into the equation given in the question, to get *a + (170 + a) = 500*. Subtracting both sides, we have *2a = 330*, and dividing both sides by 2 gives *a = 165*. Then *b = 170 + 165 = **335***.

Answer: <u>335</u>

7. Chris is 3 years older than Joseph. The sum of their ages is 79. What is Joseph's age?

This isn't totally dissimilar to the previous question, but here we are applying the ideas in context. If C is Chris's age and J is Joseph's age, then $C = J + 3$ and $C + J = 79$, then we can write $J = 79 - C$, so $C = 79 - C + 3$. Then we add C to both sides, giving $2C = 82$, so $C = 41$, and so $J = 38 - 3 = 38$.

So Joseph is **38**.

Answer: <u>38</u>

8. The diagram below shows a pictogram with information about the number of people in 3 working groups in an office. Each smiley face represents 4 people. How many more people are in Group 3 than Group 1?

Group 1	☺ ☺ (
Group 2	☺ ☺ ☺ ☺
Group 3	☺ ☺ ☺ (

We can find the number of people in each group. Group 2 has 4 full smileys. As each smiley represents 4 people, then there are 4 x 4 = 16 people in the group.

As there are 2 full smileys and a quarter in Group 1, this gives 2 ¼ x 4 = 9 and in group 3 we have: 3 ½ x 4 = 14 people.

So there are **5** more people in Group 3 than Group 1.

Answer: <u>5</u>

9. The shape below is 4cm tall and 3cm wide. What is its perimeter?

We can figure out the perimeter with no further information. Notice we can rearrange the edges of the shape (as I have done in the image below).

As such, the perimeter of a shape is the same as a rectangle that is 4cm tall and 3cm wide. Therefore, the perimeter is 4 x 2 + 3 x 2. This idea can be generally applied to many polygons formed of lines which meet at right angles.

The total perimeter, then, is **14 cm**.

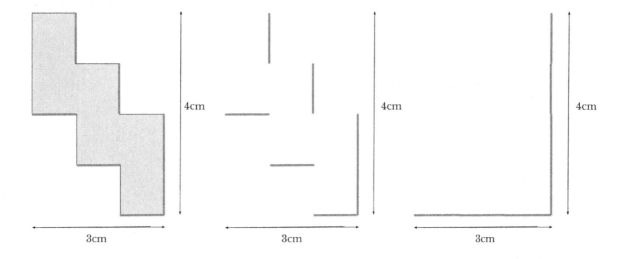

Answer: 14 cm

10. If I roll a fair dice 42 times, how many times should I expect to get a 4?

There are a few ways to think about this problem. But if I have a fair dice, no number should appear more often than any other, so I should get a four ⅙th of the time… or 42 x ⅙ = **7 times**.

Answer: 7

11. Work out 43 - 16/2 x 3.

Remember BIDMAS. With no brackets or indices, we first do $16/2 = 8$. Then we do the multiplication: $8 \times 3 = 24$. Then, finally, we do $43 - 24 = 19$.

Answer: <u>19</u>

12. We define a new mathematical operation by ($|$) where x ($|$) y means 'x-1 times y plus 3', so:

4 ($|$) 2 = (4-1) x 2 + 3 = 9

    a) What is 12 ($|$) 4?

    b) What b is such that 8 ($|$) b = 52?

    c) Find c if (c+1) ($|$) c = 67

(a)

For the first question, we can mimic the format of the question:

12 ($|$) 4 = (12-1) x 4 + 3 = 11 x 4 + 3 = 44 + 3 = **47**

Answer: <u>47</u>

(b)

For the second we again can write out (8-1) x b + 3 = 52. Simplifying and making b the subject of the equation we have 7b = 49, so b = **7**.

Answer: <u>7</u>

(c)

Finally, simplifying ((c+1)-1) x c + 3 = 67 gives us c x c = 64; so we need to find the square root of the right side of this equation, which is 8; so c = **8**.

Answer: <u>8</u>

13.Here is a list of ingredients to make 12 gluten-free brownies:

- **<u>300g cornflour</u>**
- **<u>150g sugar</u>**
- **<u>100g butter</u>**
- **<u>3 eggs</u>**
- **<u>200g chocolate</u>**

<u>How many eggs and how much chocolate do I need to make 8 brownies? Leave your answers rounded to the nearest whole number.</u>

8 = 12 x ⅔ , so we need ⅔ of everything listed here in order to make the brownies.

3 x ⅔ = 2 so we need 2 eggs.

For the chocolate as 200 is not a multiple of 3 we will need to employ the bus stop method to get 200/3 = 66 ⅔. This is of course a third of 200g. However, we need two thirds, so we multiply this number by two: 66 ⅔ x 2 = 133 ⅓.

This is 133g when rounded to the nearest whole number.

So we need **2 eggs and 133g of chocolate.**

Answer: <u>2 eggs and 133g of chocolate</u>

14. How many *squares* are there altogether in the below diagram?

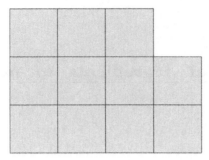

We need to be a little careful here as there are three different possible sizes of squares.

There are eleven 1x1 squares, but we also have to count the 2x2 squares. You could do this by imagining a 2x2 frame and sliding it over the diagram to judge where it will line up with the squares in the diagram. Alternatively, you can count the number of squares that could be the upper left 1x1 square in a 2x2 square, so as not to get confused or miss any. Either way, there are five 2x2 squares.

Finally, there is also one 3 x 3 square; so the answer is:

11 + 5 + 1 = **17**

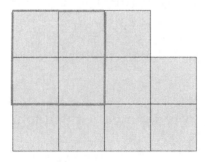

Answer: 17

15. a. What is the coordinate of the point (-2, 1) when it is reflected in the y axis?

b. What about when the point (-2, 1) is reflected in the line y = x (which is drawn for you below)?

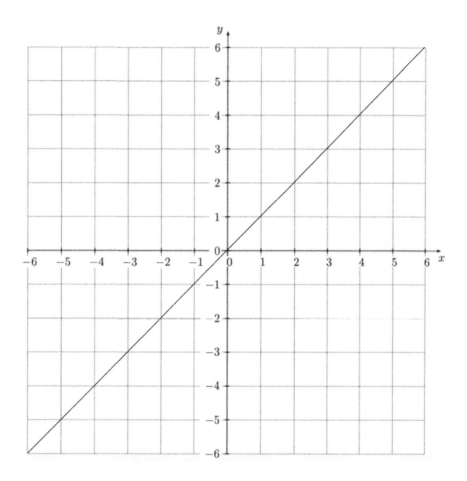

Using the diagram we can draw the point and then reflect it through the lines asked in the question.

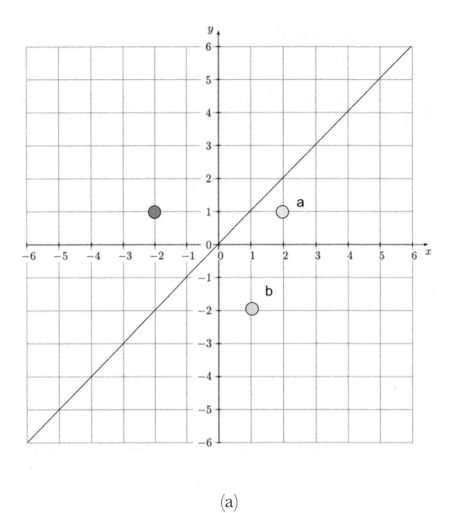

(a)

So the first coordinates the examiner is looking for (my upper-right spot above) is **(2, 1)**.

Answer: (2, 1)

(b)

And the second coordinates the examiner is looking for (my lower-right spot) is **(1, -2)**.

Answer: (1, -2)

16. The diagram below shows two parallel lines marked with arrows, being crossed by two other lines. The angles this figure forms are labelled.

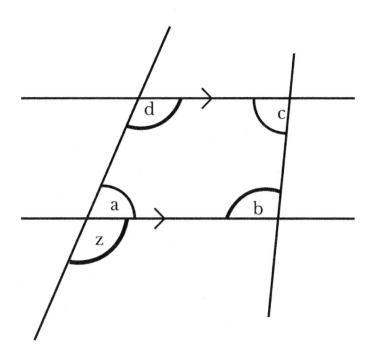

a. Given z = 120°, what is a?

b. Given b = 110°, c = 70°, what is d?

c. Finally, look at the diagram below. If now z= 63, what is d?

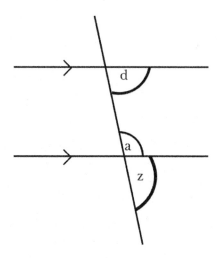

(a)

To find a, we can use the fact that angles on a straight line add up to 180. So z + a = 180; so a = 180 - 120 = **60**.

Answer: 60

(b)

Then to get d, we can use the knowledge that the interior angles of a quadrilateral add up to 360. So we have a + b + c + d = 360 and thus d = 360 - 60 - 70 - 110 = **120**.

Answer: 120

(c)

Finally, we have a more challenging question where we are expected to realise that it doesn't matter what value b or c are: angle z will always be equal to angle d. So d = **63**. Z and d are called corresponding angles.

Answer: 63

17. X is a whole number which I do not know.

a. What is the mean of X+1 and X-1?

b. What about X-1 and X+3?

(a)

There are a few approaches we could try here. If we pick a few numbers to try for X, for example X = 2, then X+1 = 3 and X-1 = 1, so their average is 2. If we try other numbers 4, 5, 10, we always find the average is the number we started with, so the answer is X. We can show this with the full algebra: to find the average of two numbers, we add them together and divide by 2, so the average of X+1 and X-1 is:

(X+1 + X-1) / 2 = (2X) / 2 = **X**. You could also think of the average of two numbers as the middle between them, which would again be X.

Answer: X

(b)

Applying the same ideas as before, we need to find the middle of X-1 and X+3, which is **X+1**. If we do the full algebra we get (X+3 + X-1) / 2 = (2X + 2) / 2 = X + 1

Answer: X + 1

18. Akmed replaces every letter of the alphabet with a number in a code. If R + A + T = 13 and T + R + A + P = 20, find the value of P.

We can notice that the only difference between the two words is that one has a P and the other doesn't. So the difference in the value of their sums is P, that is P = 20 - 13 = **7**.

Answer: 7

19. At a pizza restaurant, the waiter tells me he has run out of 8 inch wide pizzas, so I can have two 4 inch wide pizzas for the same price. The area of a pizza is approximately 3.14 x r², where r is half the width. Will I get more pizza if I take the waiter's offer?

Let's find the area of each pizza. The area of the 8 inch wide pizza is 3.14 x (8/2)²=3.14 x 16 while the area of two smaller pizzas is 2 x 3.14 x (4/2)²= 2 x 3.14 x 4 = 3.14 x 8.

We could work out 3.14 x 16 and 3.14 x 8, but clearly the first is twice as big as the second, so I would get less pizza if I take the waiter's offer. In fact, I would need four 4-inch pizzas to get the same amount!

Answer: No

20.

a. Write 36 as a product of its prime factors.

b. I'm thinking of a number which has the prime factorisation 2 x 2 x __ x 7 x 11 x __

Given that my number is a square number, what are the prime factors in the blank spaces?

c. Write the smallest square number which is even and also a multiple of 17.

(a)

First, to score the mark for section (a), we write $36 = 6 \times 6 = 2 \times 3 \times 2 \times 3$.

Answer: $36 = 2 \times 3 \times 2 \times 3$

(b)

We might notice that, when we wrote 36 as a product of its prime factors above, every prime factor appeared twice. In any square number, each prime factor must appear an even number of times. And, by the same token, if a number's prime factors each appear an even number of times, then that number must be square!

To illustrate this further: if a number's prime factors appear an even number of times, then we can split them into two identical groups, for example 2×3 and 2×3. As a result, this allows us to see that the number in question is the product of two identical numbers — in this case, 6×6. Thus the number must be square!

You wouldn't be expected to know this property of square numbers beforehand; instead, the examiner is hoping you will pick it up from the first part of the question. However, this question also demonstrates why practice can be invaluable, because students who have already encountered questions that are similar to this will be at an advantage.

At any rate, this logic allows us to fill in the blanks: they must be **7** and **11**, otherwise there would not be an even number of each prime factor.

Answer: 7 and 11

(c)

The above logic also allows us to find the answer to the last part. We know our number must have 2 and 17 as factors, and each of these must appear

$$
\begin{array}{r}
\overset{1}{3}4 \\
\times\ \ 34 \\
\hline
136 \\
+\ 1020 \\
\hline
1156 \\
\end{array}
$$

an even number of times in the prime factorisation. This gives 2 x 17 x 2 x 17 as the smallest answer.

17 x 2 = 34. And 34 x 34 = 1,156 (as I demonstrate with the column method to the left).

Answer: <u>1156</u>

Exam Paper Six

60 Minutes | 20 Questions

Practice Paper Six

1. Draw lines of symmetry on the shapes below (if they have any).

2. Below is pictured the net of a cube:

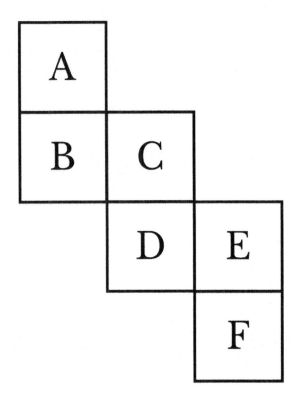

Label the following net so that when it is folded the same cube as before is made.

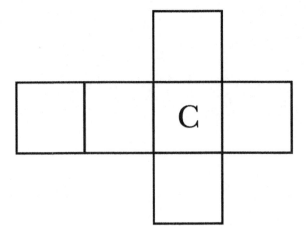

3. A cube with 4cm sides is made from cubes with 1cm sides as shown. How many of these 1cm have exactly four of their faces touching other 1cm cubes?

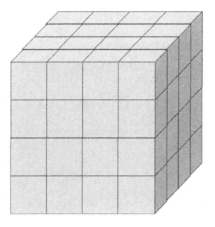

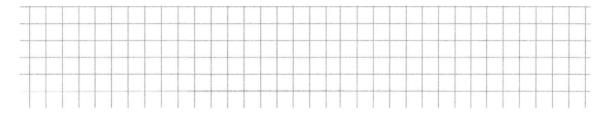

Answer:_____

4. Today is Sunday. Which of these is least likely to happen?

a) It rains tomorrow

b) It rains tomorrow and I have my umbrella

c) It rains every day next week and I bring my umbrella every day except Tuesday.

Answer:_____

5. a. Write down the number ninety-nine thousand one hundred and two using digits.

Answer:_____

b. Write down 83,414 using words.

Answer:_____

6. What is ½ of ⅙ of ⅓?

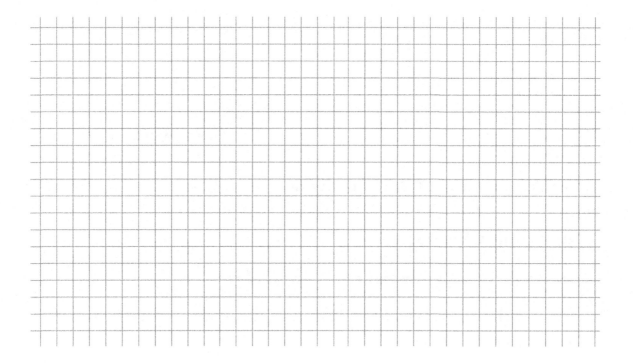

Answer:_____

. . .

7. What is 130% of 130?

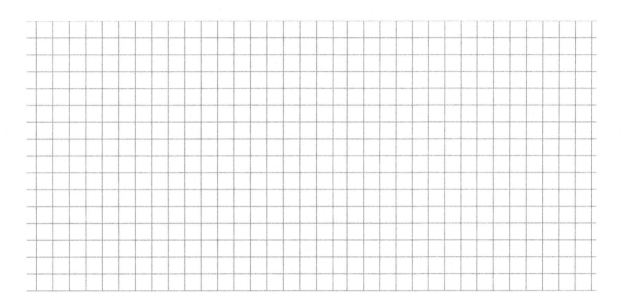

Answer:_____

8. Write the three prime numbers which multiply to make 357.

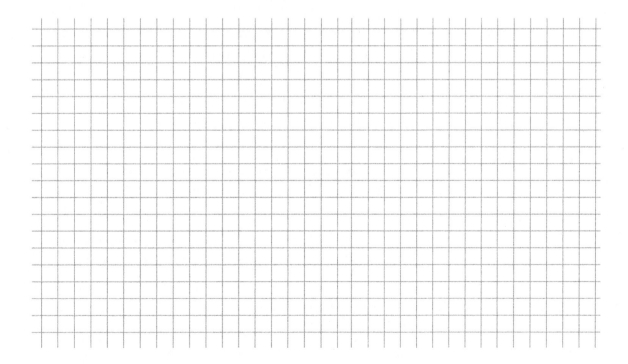

Answer:_____

9. Look at the numbers in the cloud:

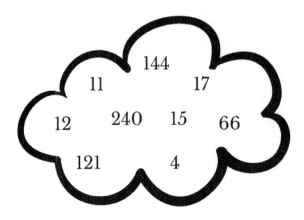

Write down all of the numbers which are:

a. Square numbers

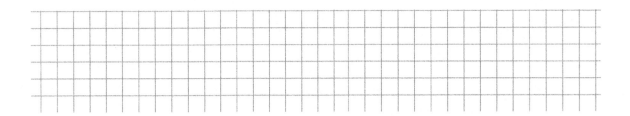

Answer:_____

b. Prime numbers

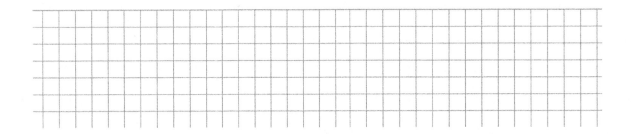

Answer:_____

c. Multiples of 11

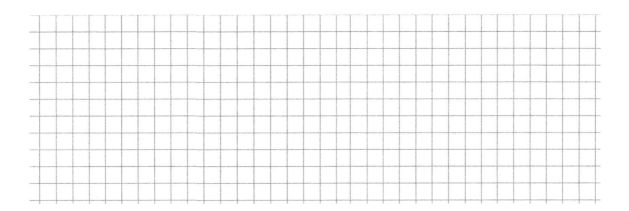

Answer:_____

10. What number goes in the square to make the equation true?

$$\frac{1}{60} + \frac{1}{30} = \frac{1}{\square}$$

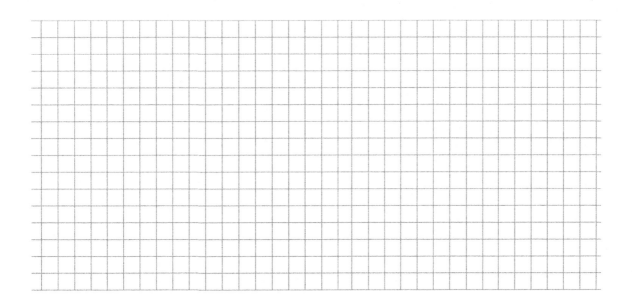

Answer:_____

11. Subtract 0.04 from 2.7

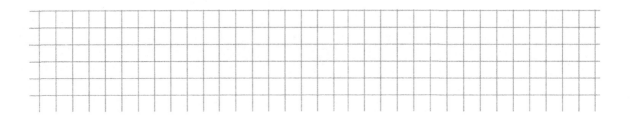

Answer:_____

12. A recipe for 14 cakes requires 350g of flour. How many cakes could I potentially make if I have 540 grams of flour?

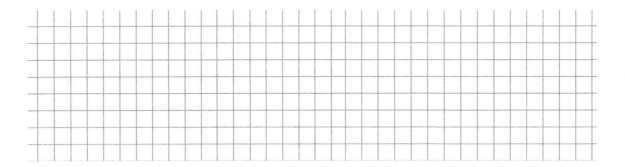

Answer:_____

13. What is the greatest odd number less that 14,000 we can write using the numbers 1 3 6 8 (use each number as many times as you like)?

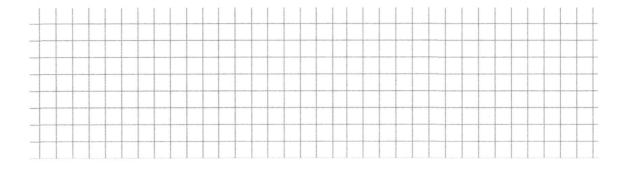

Answer:_____

14. Below is a diagram of a function machine, which changes numbers according to the rule 'multiply by 3 then subtract 4'.

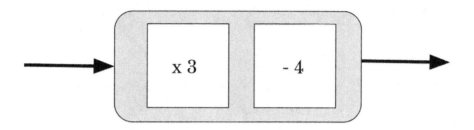

a. What is the output when we put 6 in the function machine?

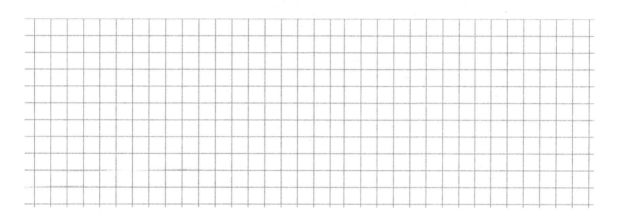

Answer:_____

b. What input would give the answer 2?

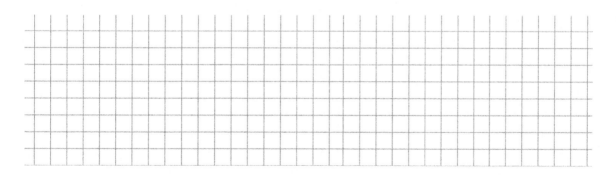

Answer:_____

15. Using the totals given, find the value of each shape.

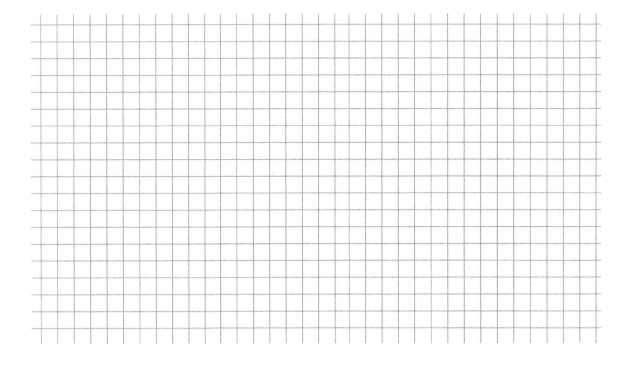

Answer:_____

16. In a fighting game, we have 4 "creatures": limpits, lampits, lompits and lumpits. We say two different groups "match" if, when they fight each other, the result is a draw. You have the following information:

- **4 lumpits match 3 limpits**
- **6 lampits match 3 lompits**
- **5 lumpits match 2 lompits**

How many lampits all in all would match a combined force of 20 lumpits and 12 lompits?

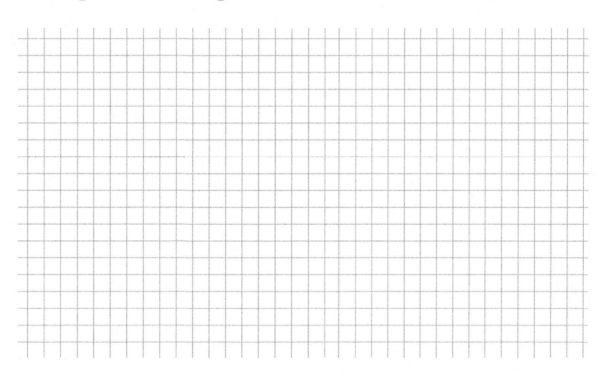

Answer:_____

17. Today is Kim's 43rd birthday. How many months old is she?

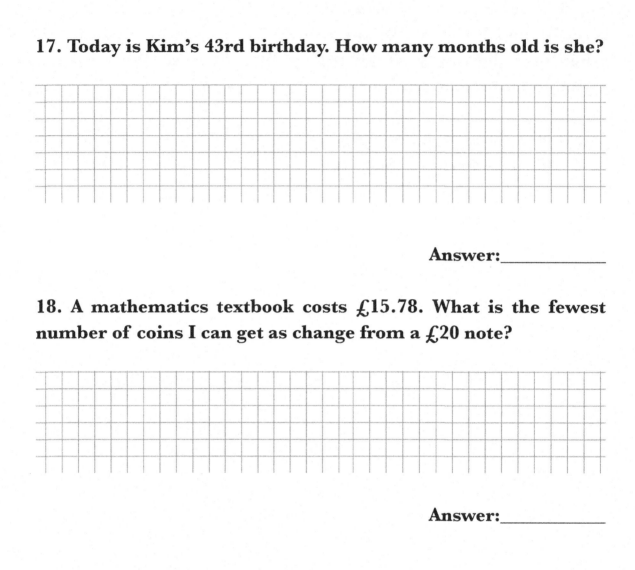

Answer:_____

18. A mathematics textbook costs £15.78. What is the fewest number of coins I can get as change from a £20 note?

Answer:_____

19. There is only one square number that is 2 less than a cube number, and it is smaller than 100. What is it?

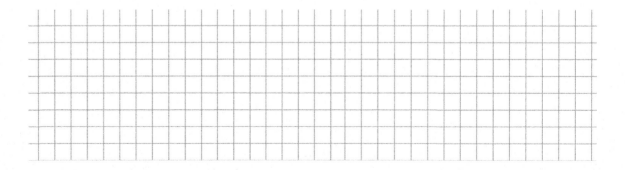

Answer:_____

20. In a triangle the largest angle is 3 times bigger than the other two, which are equal. What is the size of the largest angle?

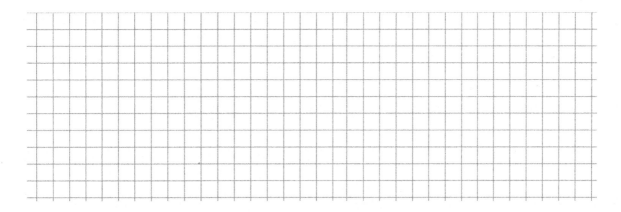

Answer:_____

Answers and Guidance

1. Draw lines of symmetry on the shapes below (if they have any).

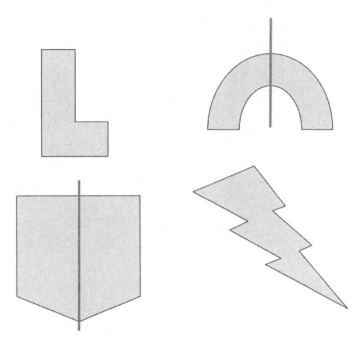

Don't be afraid to point out when a shape doesn't have lines of symmetry. There are only two lines to draw. If you are struggling identifying symmetries of shapes, try cutting out copies of these shapes and folding them to identifying lines of symmetry.

2. Below is pictured the net of a cube:

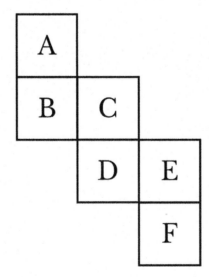

Label the following net so that, when it is, folded the same cube as before is made.

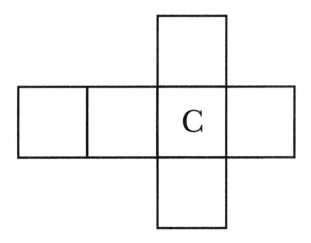

Probably the easiest way to make sure we have the answer right is to draw a sketch of the folded up cube, then work backwards to the other net. Maybe you could draw it in a single diagram, but we've reproduced it here from three different perspectives for clarity.

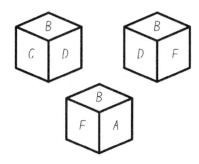

In order to know which face will have which label on the cube, we need to notice that B and D must be adjacent to C as shown. Then using your visualisation skills, after B folds to form a 90 degree angle with C, A will also fold by 90 degrees to be adjacent to C. The same holds for E, leaving F opposite C.

This was only an illustrative step. If you can visualise the folding of the first net and directly write down the labels of the second net, that's great! If you're struggling to see it, cut out some cube nets and practice folding them up.

This lets us label the new net fairly straightforwardly. In order for F to be opposite C when the net is folded, F must not be adjacent to C. Then we can fit the labels in to the new net as show below, making sure that the order will match that shown in our cube, B - D - E - A.

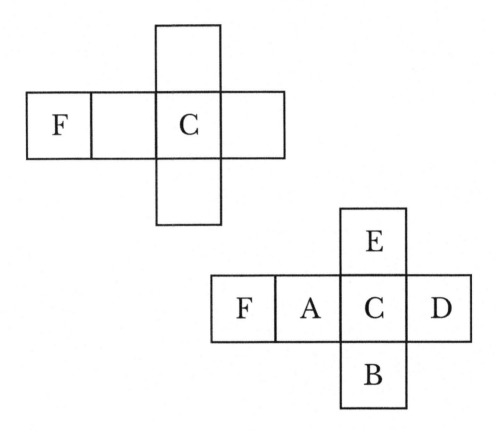

Notice that, due to the symmetries of this net, there are several other valid solutions. It is important that F always remains on the far left-hand side. But A and D could switch places, or B and E could switch places, and you would still have a correct answer. Indeed, any solution that puts E opposite to B, and D opposite to A, will technically be correct.

3. A cube with 4cm sides is made from cubes with 1cm sides as shown. How many of these 1cm have exactly four of their faces touching other 1cm cubes?

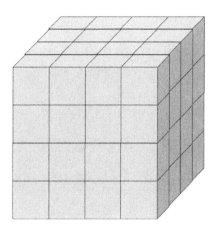

We can note that the corners (shaded in the right-hand figure) have 3 faces touching other cubes, while those cubes lying in the centre (not visible from any perspective) have all faces touching other cubes. Moreover, those in the middle of each face of the 4cm cube have 5 faces touching other cube. This leaves the cubes

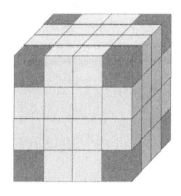

highlighted in the left-hand figure (and some others not visible from this perspective). Now we just need to count how many of these highlighted squares there are — without counting some cubes twice!

There are many sensible ways to do this. One way is to notice that each edge of the 4cm cube has 2 1cm shaded cubes. Then the answer is just twice the number of edges on a cube. One easy way to count this is to look at the nets from the previous question and count the number of edges on them! Or if you are very familiar with nets of a cube, you can draw one and count. Either way, the answer is 12 x 2 = **24**.

Answer: <u>24</u>

<u>4. Today is Sunday. Which of these is least likely to happen?</u>

<u>a) It rains tomorrow</u>

<u>b) It rains tomorrow and I have my umbrella</u>

<u>c) It rains every day next week and I bring my umbrella every day except Tuesday.</u>

This is a probability question which is purely about logic: there is no need to do any calculations.

We just need to realise that c) cannot happen if b) does not happen; and neither c) or b) can happen if a) does not happen! Thus c) cannot be more likely than b); and neither can be more likely than a)! So the answer is **c)**.

If this is not straightforward for you to see, instead consider the following question: *I have two dice: die A and die B. I roll both dice, which is more likely?*

a) Die A is a 6

b) Die A is a 6 and Die B is even

c) Die A is a 6 and Die B is not 5

If you're still struggling, write out all the possible throws of die A and die B which satisfy a), then b), then c).

Answer: <u>C</u>

5. a. Write down the number ninety-nine thousand one hundred and two using digits.

b. Write down 83,414 using words.

(a)

For the first part, we need $99,000 + 100 + 2 =$ **99,102**

Answer: 99,102

(b)

For the second part, we need to group our thousands, hundreds, tens and units. This gives **eighty-three thousand, four-hundred and fourteen.**

Answer: eighty-three thousand, four-hundred and fourteen.

6. What is ½ of ⅙ of ⅓?

Take this question in reverse. We start with ⅓ and we first want ⅙ of this. We need a number X such that $6X = ⅓$; after all, that is what it means to be ⅙ of some value. Thus we can just find $⅓ ÷ 6 = ⅓ \times ⅙ = 1/18$.

Next, we want to find $1/2$ of $1/18$.

$1/18 ÷ 2 = 1/18 \times 1/2 = 1/36$.

Thus, by using the same logic again, we find that half of $1/18$ is **1/36**. So this is our answer.

Answer: 1/36

7. What is 130% of 130?

We can split this up into first finding 30% of 130 then adding this to 100% of 130 (100% of 130 of course being 130).

30% of 130 is $^3/_{10}$ x 130 = 3 x 13 = 39; so the answer is 130 + 39 = **169**.

The alternative is to multiply 130 by 1.3, which will yield the same answer, as demonstrated by the column method.

$$
\begin{array}{r}
130 \\
\times\ 1.3 \\
\hline
390 \\
+\ 1300 \\
\hline
169.0
\end{array}
$$

Answer: 169

8. Write the three prime numbers which multiply to make 357.

If you remembered some of our rules from earlier, you could note that 3 + 5 + 7 is a multiple of 3, and so 3 is a factor of 357. Alternatively it makes sense to try the smaller primes first. Dividing by 3 we get 357 / 3 = 119 which is not easy to guess the factors of.

We could note that 357 = 350 + 7 = 7 x 5 x 10 + 7, so 7 is another factor, and this gives us 357 = 7 x (5 x 10 + 1) = 7 x 51. We already know 3 also divides 357, thus we divide 51 by 3 to get the final prime factor 17.

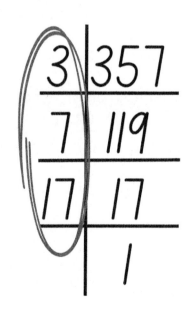

Alternatively, we could use our step ladder method, which involves dividing 357 by the smallest prime number possible — then doing the same with the result — until you can do so no longer. The digits on the left-hand side are the prime numbers that multiply to make 357.

Answer: <u>3, 7 and 17</u>

9. Look at the numbers in the cloud:

Write down all of the numbers which are:

a. Square numbers

b. Prime numbers

c. Multiples of 11

(a)

First we should recognise **4** = 2 x 2. Slightly more tricky to catch are 11 x 11 = **121** and 12 x 12 = **144**. You should at least know the square numbers up to 100. This leaves you only 3 numbers to check, the largest of which is 240. This figure is smaller than 16 x 16 = 256 and larger than 15 x 15 = 225, and thus is not a square number.

Answer: <u>4, 121, 144</u>

(b)

We can discount all the even numbers as 2 is not in the cloud. We identified that $121 = 11 \times 11$, so this is not prime. This leaves only 11, 15 and 17, and we should be able to see that 15 is a multiple of 5 as it ends in a 5. This leaves us with just **11 and 17**.

Answer: <u>11 and 17</u>

(c)

Clearly **11**, the double digits **66** $= 6 \times 11$ and we already know **121** $= 11 \times$ 11. These are the only answers.

Answer: <u>11, 66 and 121</u>

10. What number goes in the square to make the equation true?

$$\frac{1}{60} + \frac{1}{30} = \frac{1}{\square}$$

The easiest way to see the answer is to write all the fractions on the left hand side with the same denominator $\frac{1}{60} + \frac{1}{30} = \frac{1}{60} + \frac{2}{60} = \frac{3}{60} = \frac{1}{20}$. So the number in the box is **20**.

Answer: <u>20</u>

11. Subtract 0.04 from 2.7

Write 2.7 as 2.70, then 2.70 - 0.04 = **2.66**

Answer: 2.66

12. A recipe for 14 cakes requires 350g of flour. How many cakes could I potentially make if I have 540 grams of flour?

We can work out that one cake requires 350 / 14 = 25g of flour. Then 540 / 25 = 21 with remainder 15. Thus we can make up to **21** cakes with this amount of flour.

Answer: 21

13. What is the greatest odd number less that 14,000 we can write using the numbers 1 3 6 8 (use each number as many times as you like)?

If the number must be odd, then we just need it to end in 1 or 3. If the number started with 6 or 8 then we could only pick a 4 digit number, but if we start with 1, we can have a 5 digit number, so long as our second digit is 3.

Then to make the number as large as possible, we just need to add 8s everywhere else (as this is the largest number) — that is, except for when it comes to the final digit, which should be 3. So the answer is **13,883**.

Answer: <u>13,883</u>

14. Below is a diagram of a function machine, which changes numbers according to the rule 'multiply by 3 then subtract 4'.

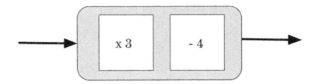

a. What is the output when we put 6 in the function machine?

b. What input would give the answer 2?

(a)

When we have an output and want to find an input, we need to follow the operations of the machine from left to right. 6 x 3 =18 and then 18 - 4 = **14**.

Answer: <u>14</u>

(b)

When we have an output and want to find an input, we need to work backwards from right to left, using the inverse of the operations. So we take the output 2 and add 4, this gives 6. Then we divide by 3 to get the answer, which is **2**.

You can check this is in fact the input by putting it back through the function machine and checking the output is 2.

Answer: <u>2</u>

15. Using the totals given, find the value of each shape.

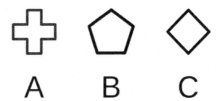

This is definitely a tougher question. We will call the shapes A, B and C as labelled below, as this makes it easier to refer to them.

A   B   C

This is definitely a tough question but similar questions have appeared on real exams. For ease we will label each shape with a letter and rewrite the equations using algebra

A + B + C = 6

2A + C = 5

2B + A = 8

Then we can use the third equation to write:

A = 8 - 2B

And the second equation to write

$$C = 5 - 2A = 5 - 2 \times (8 - 2B) = 4B - 11$$

Now we have A and C in terms of B, we can sub these into the first equation:

$$8 - 2B + B + 4B - 11 = 6$$

Simplifying:

$$3B - 3 = 6$$

Thus **B = 3**.

We can now use our previous equations for A and C in terms of B, to get **A = 2** and **C = 1**.

Answer: <u>A=2 B=3 C=1</u>

16. In a fighting game, we have 4 "creatures": limpits, lampits, lompits and lumpits. We say two different groups "match" if, when they fight each other, the result is a draw. You have the following information:

a) 4 lumpits match 3 limpits

b) 6 lampits match 3 lompits

c) 5 lumpits match 2 lompits

How many lampits all in all would match a combined force of 20 lumpits and 12 lompits?

We again can first convert the problem into an algebra question. We will use the letters A I O U for lampits, limpits, lompits and lumpits respectively. Then we have the equalities:

$4U = 3I$

$6A = 3O$

$5U = 2O$

Then we want to write $20U + 12O$ in terms of A. Note that $6A=3O$ can be simplified to $2A=O$.

Since $5U = 2O$ we have $20U = 8O$ and thus $20U + 12O = 20O = 20 \times (2A) = \underline{\textbf{40A}}$.

Here's another way of working this through:

We know that '6 lampits match 3 lompits.'

If we have 12 lompits – that is, four times as many – we will need four times as many lampits. 6 x 4 = 24 lampits.

But we also need more lampits to match the 20 lumpits also in play.

However, we haven't been told directly how many lampits match how many lumpits, so we need to work this out.

We have been told that '5 lumpits match 2 lompits.'

From this we can infer that 15 lumpits match 6 lompits: I am simply multiplying both figures by 3.

And we can also infer from '6 lampits match 3 lompits' that 12 lampits match 6 lompits.

With this information, we can see that 15 lumpits = 12 lampits.

The question, however, is asking us how many lampits we need to match 20 lumpits.

If 15 lumpits = 12 lampits, then we know that 20 lumpits = 16 lampits (we are simply multiplying both 15 and 12 by 1⅓).

So the total number of lampits needed to match 20 lumpits and 12 lompits = 24 + 16 = **40 lampits**.

             Answer: 40 lampits

17. Today is Kim's 43rd birthday. How many months old is she?

We know it's been exactly 43 years since Kim was born. There are 12 months in a year so she has been alive for 43 x 12 = 516.

             Answer: 516

18. A mathematics textbook costs £15.78. What is the fewest number of coins I can get as change from a £20 note?

The possible coins are £2, £1, 50p, 20p, 10p, 5p, 2p and 1p. The change we get from £20 is 20 - 15.78 = £4.22. We should use £2 instead of £1 coins so this gives £4 with 2 coins; and to get the remaining 22p we can use a 20p and 2p; so it can be done with 4 coins.

So our answer is **4 coins**!

             Answer: 4

19. There is only one square number that is 2 less than a cube number, and it is smaller than 100. What is it?

The cube numbers less than 100 are 1, 8, 27, 64. So we subtract 2 from each of these. This gives -1, 6, 25 and 62 as the only possible candidates. The only square is **25**, so this is the answer.

Answer: 25

20. In a triangle the largest angle is 3 times bigger than the other two, which are equal. What is the size of the largest angle?

Let x be the size of the smaller two angles. Then the biggest angle is size 3x. Since we know the angles in a triangle add to 180, we have 3x + x + x =180 so 5x = 180 which means x = 36.

Then the biggest angle is size 3 x 36 = **108**.

Answer: 108

Exam Paper Seven

60 Minutes | 20 Questions

Practice Paper Seven

1. Work out $2\frac{2}{3} + 1\frac{7}{5}$

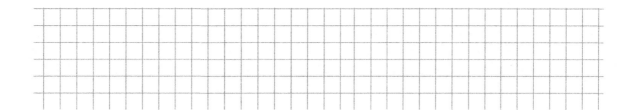

Answer:_____

2. What number is halfway between 11.9 and 11.99.

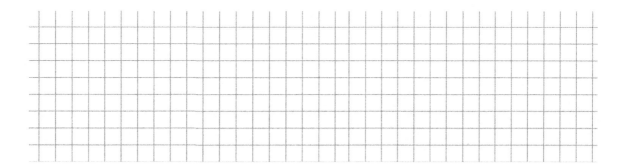

Answer:_____

3. Write these numbers in order from smallest to largest

5.23, 6, 1.7, 11, 3.54, 6.01

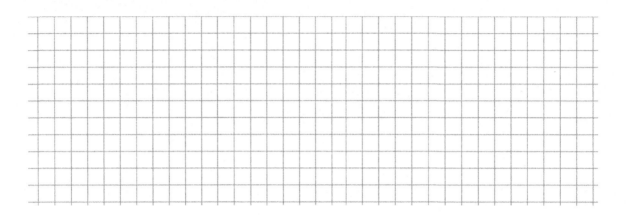

Answer:_____

4. A number is palindromic when it is the same written forwards as backwards, for example 34543.

How many positive palindromic numbers are there that are smaller than 150?

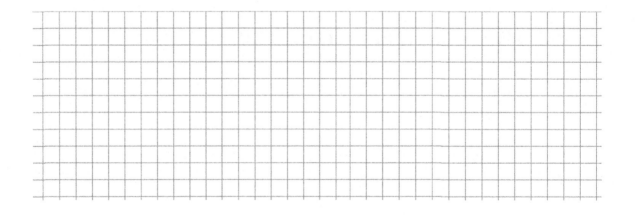

Answer:_____

5. 2 apples and 5 grapes cost 87p and 4 apples and a grape cost £1.65. What does one apple cost?

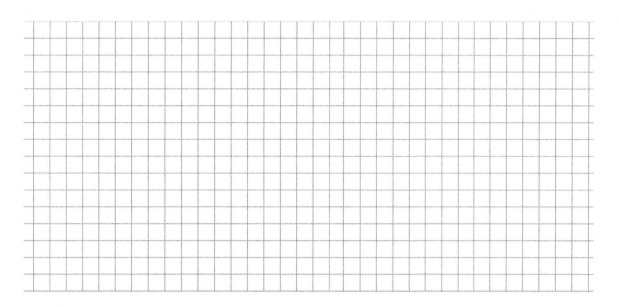

Answer:_____

6. Jules makes a drink for her bar using a mix of orange juice and lemonade. She uses twice as much lemonade as orange juice. If she uses 868ml of lemonade, how much of the drink will she make in total?

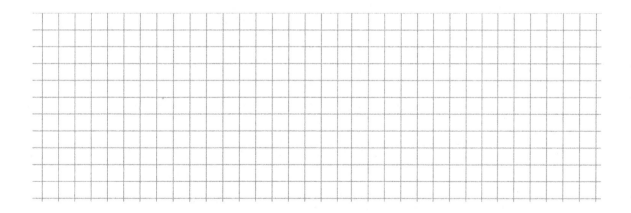

Answer:_____

7. Mas is 21 years and 3 months old.

Niamh is 25 years and 1 months old.

Ellen is 22 years and 11 months old.

What is their average age in years and months?

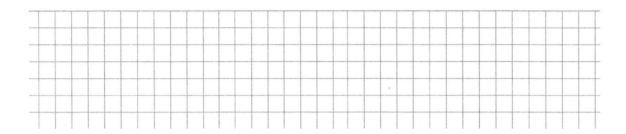

Answer:_____

8. Ben wants to order some Christmas cards from an online company.

Below is a graph where the number of cards in an order is shown on the x axis, and the y axis shows the costs in £ of the order.

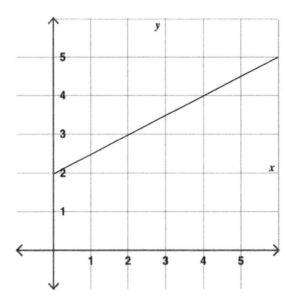

a) Shipping an order of any size costs £2. How much does each card cost?

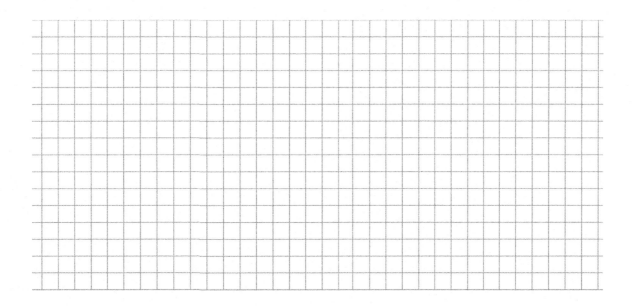

Answer:_____

b) How much would an order of 5 cards cost?

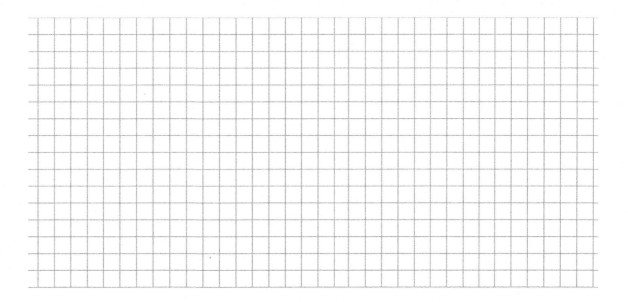

Answer:_____

9. Consider the shape below.

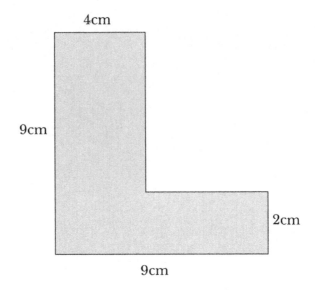

a. What is the area of this shape?

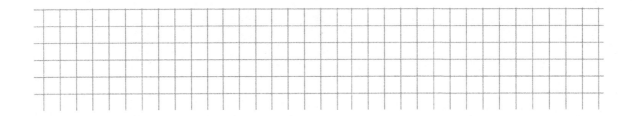

Answer:_____

b. What is the perimeter of this shape?

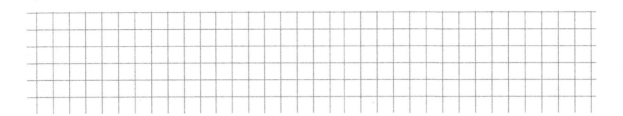

Answer:_____

10. We can use 4 1cm width squares to make a 2cm square as shown below:

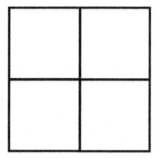

How many equilateral triangles with a side length of 1cm do we need in order to make an equilateral triangle with side lengths of 3cm?

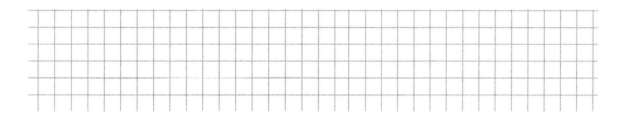

Answer:_____

11. A car sets off from London to Edinburgh – which is a journey of 400 miles in total – with 50 litres of fuel in the tank. Its average speed is 60 mph. The car uses 0.1 litres of fuel per mile.   How much fuel is left in the car when it reaches Edinburgh?

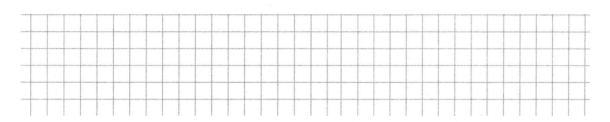

Answer:_____

12. Consider the below network map of roads between towns.

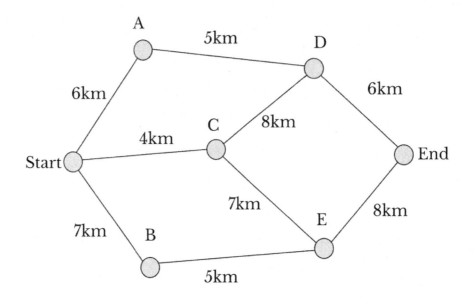

a. What is the shortest path from Start to End?

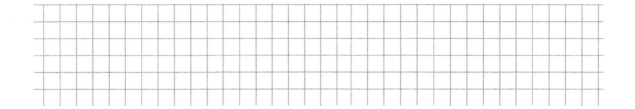

Answer:_____

b. What is the length of the shortest path from Start to End?

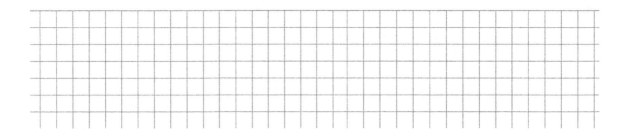

Answer:_____

13. How many hours were there in the year 2017? Keep in mind that 2000 was a leap year.

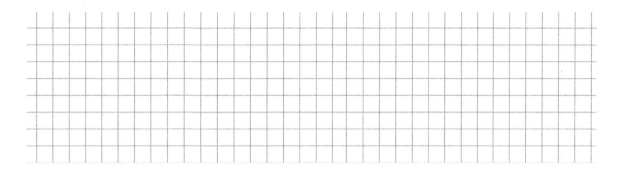

Answer:_____

14. A large crate contains 80 cartons of juice. Each layer of the large crate contains 16 cartons of juice. How many layers are there in the large crate?

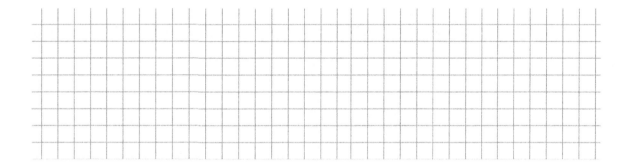

Answer:_____

15. What's 10% of 20% of 30% of 111,000

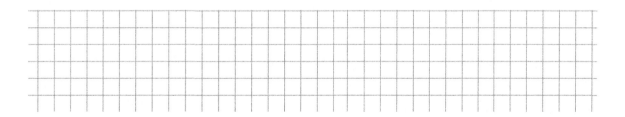

Answer:_____

16. The diagram shows two parallel lines labeled with arrows, and angles a, b, c caused by a third line intersecting them. Two other right angles are shown where a fourth line intersects the parallel lines.

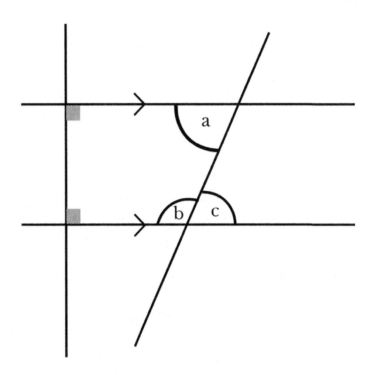

a. Given a = 60, find b and c

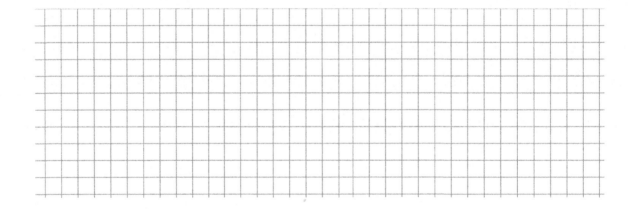

Answer:_____

b. Now consider this similar diagram, where only the fourth line has moved. Given a = 60, what is angle c?

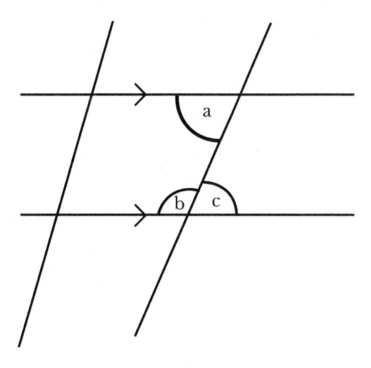

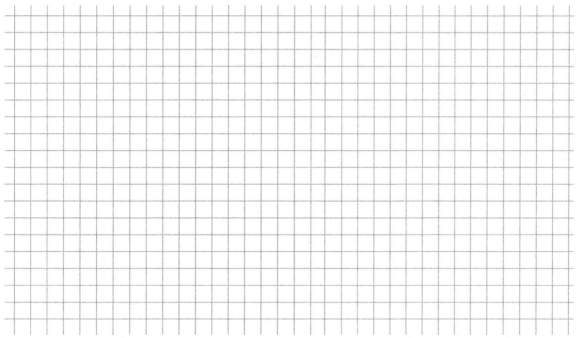

Answer:_____

c. Now finally consider the below diagram. If a = 50, what is c?

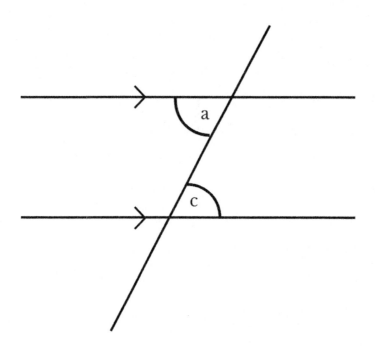

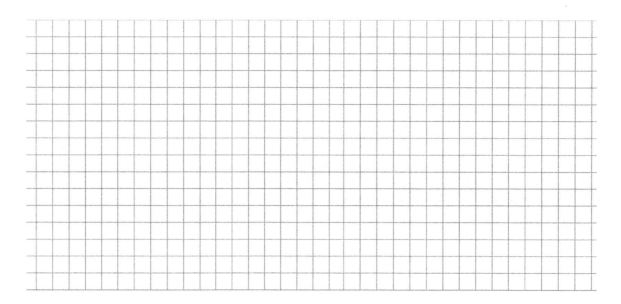

Answer:_____

17. Kate designs a rug which is hexagonal in shape and is split into 6 identical triangles as shown below.

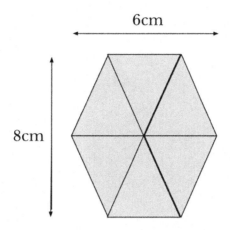

Find the area of the rug.

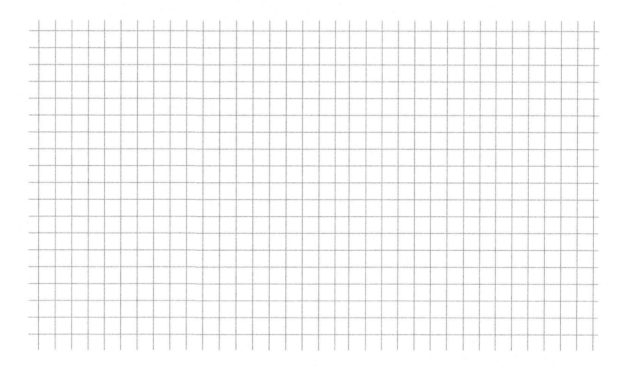

Answer:_____

18. Write down the order of rotational symmetry of the following shapes.

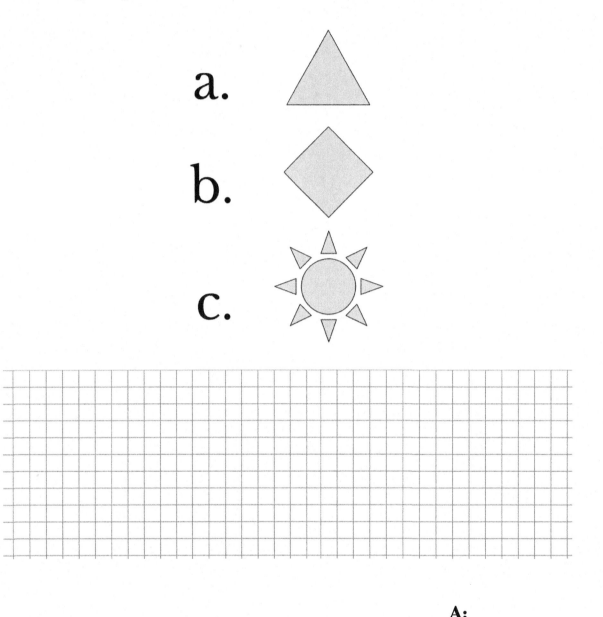

A:_____

B:_____

C:_____

19. Pam and Phil start on opposite ends A and B of a track and run to and fro. Pam takes 5 seconds to run from one end to the other. Phil takes 6 seconds to run from one end to the other. How many times do they pass each other in 60 seconds?

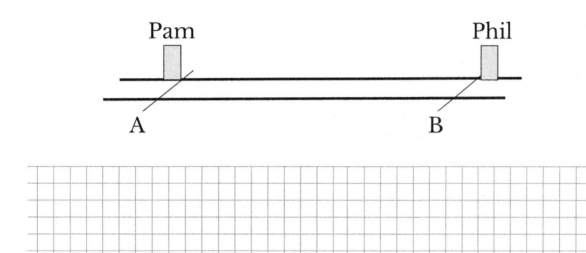

Answer:_____

20. There are 21 people in each class in an elementary school. The school has 3 classes, A, B and C.

The average height of pupils in Class A is 1.3m

The average height of pupils in Class B is 1.2m

The average height of pupils in Class C is 1.1m

Jim joins the school, and his height is 1.4m

What is the average height of a pupil in the school? Leave your answer as a mixed number.

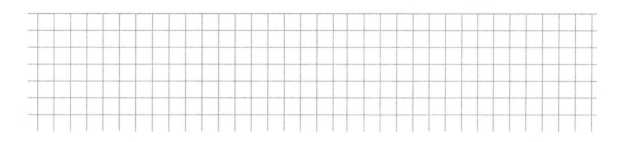

Answer:_____

Answers and Guidance

1. Work out $2\frac{2}{3} + 1\frac{7}{5}$

We need to notice the second term is an improper fraction, so we rewrite the mixed number as $1\frac{7}{5} = 2\frac{2}{5}$.

Then we can add the integers and the fraction parts, so:

$2\frac{2}{3} + 2\frac{2}{5} = 2 + 2 + \frac{2}{3} + \frac{2}{5} = 4 + \frac{6}{15} + \frac{10}{15} = 4 + \frac{16}{15} = 5\frac{1}{15}$

Answer: $5\frac{1}{15}$

2. What number is halfway between 11.9 and 11.99.

The easiest way to find the middle of two numbers is to add them and divide by two, so we need to find $(11.9 + 11.99)/2 = (23.89)/2 = \mathbf{11.945}$.

Answer: 11.945

3. Write these numbers in order from smallest to largest

5.23, 6, 1.7, 11, 3.54, 6.01

We have discussed these types of questions before so look back over previous answers if you are struggling. The answer is **1.7, 3.54, 5.23, 6, 6.01, 11**

Answer: 1.7, 3.54, 5.23, 6, 6.01, 11

4. A number is palindromic when it is the same written forwards as backwards, for example 34543.

How many positive palindromic numbers are there that are smaller than 150?

Notice all of the single digit numbers are palindromic, 1,2,3,...9 so we have 9 palindromic numbers right off the bat — we do not count 0 as we are looking for positive numbers. Then all the multiples of 11 below 100 are also palindromic numbers. 11,22,33,...,99 so that is another 9.

Then, over 100, our numbers must start in 1, so they must also end in 1. Below 150, this only leaves 101, 111, 121, 131, 141. That is 5 more numbers.

So we have 9 + 9 + 5 = 23. So the answer is **23**.

Answer: 23

5. 2 apples and 5 grapes cost 87p and 4 apples and a grape cost £1.65. What does one apple cost?

We can use algebra to see more clearly what is going on here. Let A be an apple and G be a grape. Then:

$2A + 5G = 87$

$4A + G = 165$

So from the second equation we can write $G = 165 - 4A$

Subbing this in to the first equation we have:

$2A + 5 \times (165 - 4A) = 87$

$2A + 825 - 20A = 87$

$18A = 738$

$A = 41$

So the apple costs **41p.**

Answer: 41p

6. Jules makes a drink for her bar using a mix of orange juice and lemonade. She uses twice as much lemonade as orange juice. If she uses 868ml of lemonade, how much of the drink will she make in total?

First we work out how much orange juice she will use. This will be half as much as the amount of lemonade, so 868 / 2 = 434. Then the total amount of liquid is:

434 x 3 = **1302ml,** so this is the answer.

Answer: 1302ml

7. Mas is 21 years and 3 months old.

Niamh is 25 years and 1 months old.

Ellen is 22 years and 11 months old.

What is their average age in years and months?

We can write each of their ages as a mixed number.

Mas is $21\ ^3/_{12}$ years old, Niamh is $25\ ^1/_{12}$ and Ellen is $22\ ^{11}/_{12}$ years old. We now add all these up to get $68\ ^{15}/_{12} = 69\ ^3/_{12}$ now to get the average we just need to divide this by 3 to get **$23^1/_{12}$**.

Answer: 23 years and 1 month

8. Ben wants to order some Christmas cards from an online company.

Below is a graph where the number of cards in an order is shown on the x axis, and the y axis shows the costs in £ of the order.

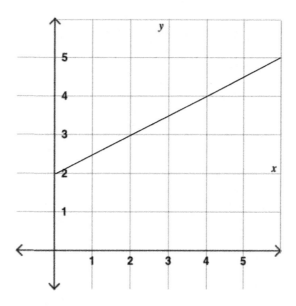

a. Shipping an order of any size costs £2. How much does each card cost?

b. How much would an order of 5 cards cost?

(a)

We can find the cost of a single card by looking at an order of one card, then subtracting the shipping costs. Reading from the graph we can see that an order with a single card costs £2.50 in total; so subtracting the shipping cost, we can see that a card costs **50p**.

Answer: 50p

(b)

We can work this out either by reading the graph, or by using the fact that each card costs 50p. An order of 5 cards costs £2 + 50p x 5 = **£4.50.**

9. Consider the shape below.

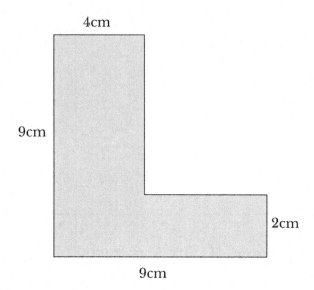

a. What is the area of this shape?

b. What is the perimeter of this shape?

(a)

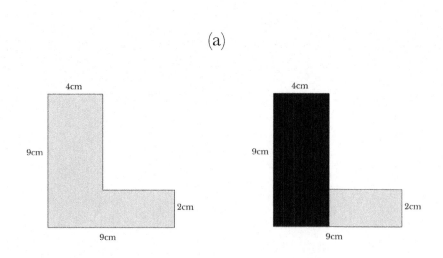

We split the shape into two smaller rectangles

The area of the darker rectangle is clearly 4 x 9 = 36cm² while the lighter rectangle has height 2cm and width 9 - 4 = 5cm and thus has area 10cm². Thus the total area is **46cm²**.

Answer: 46cm²

(b)

We can find the perimeter by labelling the lengths of all the missing sides like we did with the light grey rectangle.

The sum of all these is 9 + 4 + 7 + 5 + 2 + 9 = 36. Alternatively we could note that this shape must have the same perimeter as a 9cm by 9cm square, which is 9 x 4 = **36cm**.

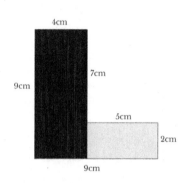

Answer: 36cm

10. We can use 4 1cm width squares to make a 2cm square as shown below:

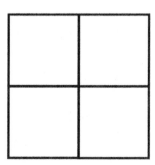

How many equilateral triangles with a side length of 1cm do we need in order to make an equilateral triangle with side lengths of 3cm?

We could achieve this by drawing things out. As below, the diagram shows a total of 9 triangles.

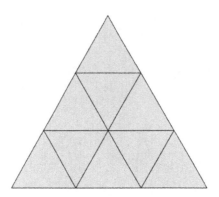

Answer: <u>9</u>

11. A car sets off from London to Edinburgh – which is a journey of 400 miles in total – with 50 litres of fuel in the tank. Its average speed is 60 mph. The car uses 0.1 litres of fuel per mile. How much fuel is left in the car when it reaches Edinburgh?

In this question we need to find the important information, which is that we will travel 400 miles and use 0.1 litres of fuel per mile. Thus we will use 40 litres of fuel during the journey.

As a result, there will be 50 - 40 = **10 litres** of fuel left in the tank.

Answer: <u>10 litres</u>

12. Consider the below network map of roads between towns.

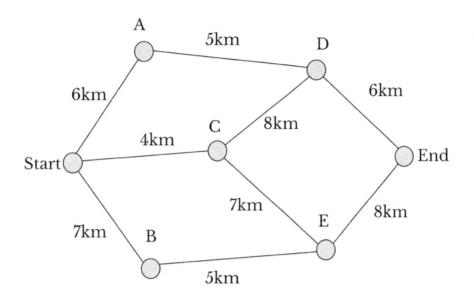

a. What is the shortest path from Start to End?

b. What is the length of the shortest path from Start to End?

(a)

The shortest path is **Start - A - D - End**. This is quite straightforward to see if you test out a couple of options.

Answer: <u>Start - A - D - End</u>

(b)

The length of this path is 6 + 5 + 6 = **17km.**

Answer: <u>17km</u>

13. How many hours were there in the year 2017? Keep in mind that 2000 was a leap year.

The year 2017 was not a leap year. Leap years are every 4 years; the year 2000 was a leap year. Since 2017 is odd, this can't be a leap year. So there are 365 days in this year. Since there are 24 hours in a day, there are 365 x 24 = **8760** hours in the year 2017.

Answer: <u>8760</u>

<u>14. A large crate contains 80 cartons of juice. Each layer of the large crate contains 16 cartons of juice. How many layers are there in the large crate?</u>

Here we just need to convert the word problem into a division problem. If there are 80 cartons in total and 16 in a layer, then we need 80 / 16 = **5 layers** to form a crate.

Answer: <u>5 layers</u>

<u>15. What's 10% of 20% of 30% of 111,000</u>

We need to not panic here and simply work backwards! We can find 30% of 111,000 easily by writing the percentage as a fraction $^3/_{10}$ x 111,000 = $^{333000}/_{10}$ = 33,300. In the same way we can find 20% of this, which is 210 x 33,300 = 66,60010 = 6660. Finally 10% of this is just one tenth of 6660 which is **666**.

Answer: <u>666</u>

<u>16. The diagram shows two parallel lines labeled with arrows, and angles a, b, c caused by a third line intersecting them. Two</u>

other right angles are shown where a fourth line intersects the parallel lines.

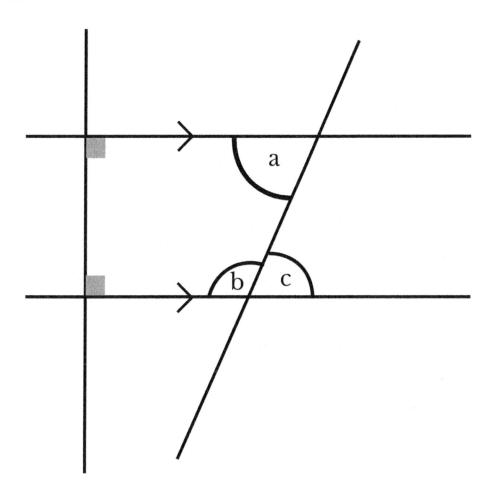

a. Given a = 60, find b and c

b. Now consider this similar diagram, where only the fourth line has moved. Given a = 60, what is angle c?

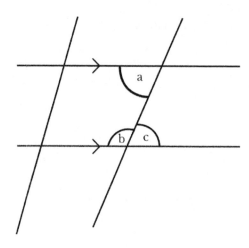

c. Now finally consider the below diagram. If a = 50, what is c?

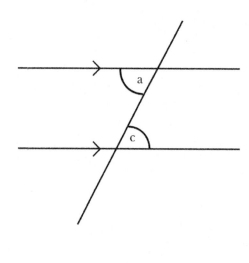

(a)

We can use the fact that angles in a quadrilateral add up to 360. So if we have two right angles and a = 60 then b = 360 - 90 - 90 - 60 = 120. Then as angles on a straight line add up to 180, we have c = 180 - b = 60.

Answer: b = 120 & c = 60

(b)

For the second part we can notice that nothing has changed the angles a, b or c, so c=60 still.

Answer: 60

(c)

Finally we should conclude that no matter where that fourth line is, angle a = c, so if a = 50 then c = **50**.

Answer: 50

17. Kate designs a rug which is hexagonal in shape and is split into 6 identical triangles as shown below.

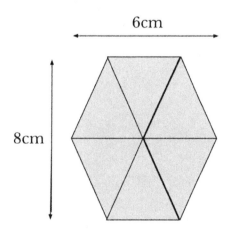

Find the area of the rug.

Given the rug is formed of 6 identical triangles, we can find the area of one of the triangles and multiply this by 6. The width of the hexagon is 6cm, and we can notice that its widest point is formed from two bases of the 6 triangles. Thus the base of one triangle must be 6 x ½ = 3cm. The height of the hexagon is 8cm and we can see visually that this must be twice the height of one of the triangles. Thus each triangle has a height of 4cm. So the area of one triangle is ½ x base x height = ½ x 3 x 4 = 6.

We have 6 triangles so the total area is **36cm²**.

Answer: 36cm²

18. Write down the order of rotational symmetry of the following shapes.

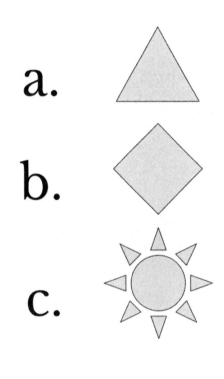

a.

b.

c.

The order of rotational symmetry is the number of angles which we can rotate the shape by and have exactly the same shape. Every shape can be rotated by 0 or 360 degrees (which is the same thing) and thus every shape has at least an order of 1.

(a)

Looking at A we can see it is an equilateral triangle: all 3 angles are the same and 3 sides are the same length, and thus it has order **3** rotational symmetry. We can rotate it by 120, 240 and 360 degrees.

Answer: 3

(b)

B has 4 sides that are the same and 4 angles that are the same, and so has order **4** rotational symmetry. We can rotate it by 90, 180, 270 and 360 degrees.

Answer: 4

(c)

Finally we have 8 points for this figure, and thus we can rotate it 8 times and it will look identical. So C has order **8**.

Answer: 8

19. Pam and Phil start on opposite ends A and B of a track and run to and fro. Pam takes 5 seconds to run from one end to the other. Phil takes 6 seconds to run from one end to the other. How many times do they pass each other in 60 seconds?

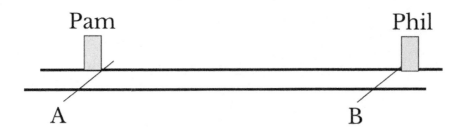

This question definitely requires some out the box thinking, and is in fact a LCM question in disguise. We can work out that in 60 seconds, Phil will get from one end of the track to the other 10 times, while Pam will 12 times. Every time Phil gets from one end of the track, he must pass Pam, so the number of times they pass is at least 10. The same is also true for Pam. There is no way she can get from A to B without passing Phil coming the other way. So the number of times is at least 12. There is no way that Phil could pass her again before she gets to the end of the track, as he is slower than her. We might stop there and conclude that the answer is 12. However, if they meet at one of the ends rather than somewhere in between, this will count for both the pass on the forward trip from A to B, and the backward trip from B to A. So we need to subtract 1 every time this happens.

The LCM of 6 and 5 is 30. So every 30 seconds we should see Phil and Pam both at one of the ends. As a result, after 30 seconds Pam has run from one end to the other 6 times, while Phil has run from one end to the other 5 times. So Pam will be on the same end (A) as she has run to and fro an even number of times, while Phil is at the opposite end to which he started (which is A) as he had run an odd number of times. So they will be at the same end and thus we must subtract 1.

So the answer is **11**.

Answer: 11

20. There are 21 people in each class in an elementary school. The school has 3 classes, A, B and C.

The average height of pupils in Class A is 1.3m

The average height of pupils in Class B is 1.2m

The average height of pupils in Class C is 1.1m

Jim joins the school, and his height is 1.4m

What is the average height of a pupil in the school? Leave your answer as a mixed number.

We can first work out the average height before Jim joins. As there are an equal number of pupils in each class, this is (1.3 + 1.2 + 1.1) / 3 = 3.6 / 3 = 1.2.

Now Jim has joined the school, there are 64 pupils in the school. So we can work out the new average by taking the sum of all the 63 children's heights, and then adding Jim's and dividing by 64. We know that the 63 children must have a total height of 63 x 1.2, as this would be the total which we divide by 63 to get the mean 1.2. So 63 x 1.2 is the same as finding 120% of 63 which is 63 + 63 x $^2/_{10}$ = 75.6.

Then we add Jim's height of 1.4 to get a total of 77.

So the answer is $^{77}/_{64}$ which is **1$^{13}/_{64}$** as a mixed number.

Answer: 1$^{13}/_{64}$

Exam Paper Eight

60 Minutes | 20 Questions

Practice Paper Eight

1. The distance from London to Edinburgh is 400 miles. 5 miles is approximately 8 kilometres.

Calculate the approximate distance from London to Edinburgh in kilometres.

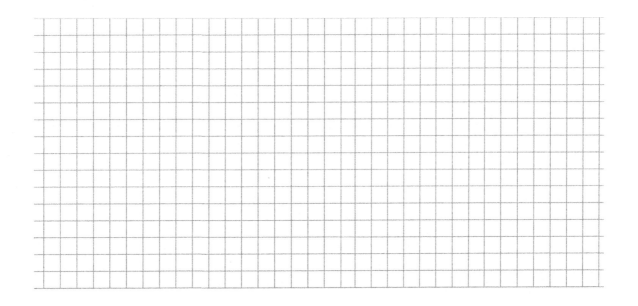

Answer:_____

2. Marcus thinks of a number (in Roman numerals).

He adds IX and multiplies by V. His answer is LV.

What was his number? Write your answer in Roman numerals.

Answer:_____

3. How many odd numbers between 1000 and 1300 contain at least one 2 in their digits?

Answer:_____

4. In a gym there are 72 people. If 25% are running on a treadmill, and ⅓ are lifting weights, how many are doing something else?

Answer:_____

5. If a triangle has sides which are all whole numbers, and its perimeter is 11cm. How many different triangles with these properties are possible?

Be careful! Remember that the nature of a triangle is such that the length of no two sides can add up to less than the length of the third. For instance, a triangle with sides 1, 2, 4 does not exist, as 1+2=3 < 4.

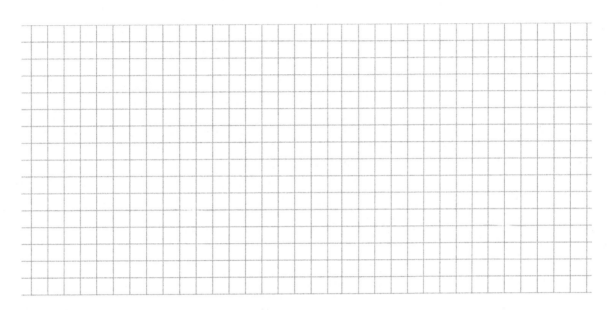

Answer:_____

6. Which of the numbers below gives the best estimate of the amount of milk in a bowl of cereal:

1ml   10ml   100ml   1L   10L

Answer:_____

7. A box of gloves contains 4 pairs of gloves. What is the smallest number of gloves I need to take out of the box to guarantee that I have both a left-hand glove and a right hand glove?

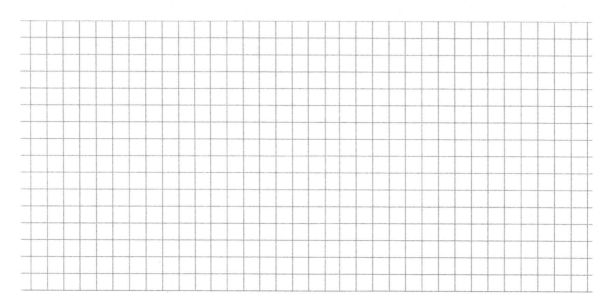

Answer:_____

8. I take my dog on a walk. She walks at 4km/h. Tibbles the cat walks 75% as fast as my dog. How long does it take Tibbles to walk 8km? Leave your answer in hours and minutes.

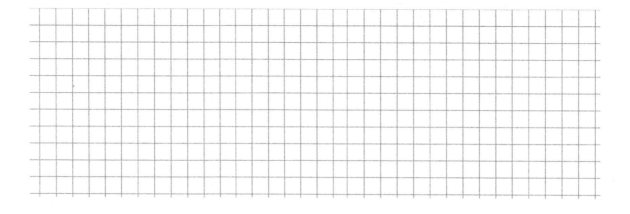

Answer:_____

9. In the Land of Nee, there are 3 types of coin. In order of value – from most valuable to least valuable – they are the triangular coin, the square coin, and the circular coin. We know the following information:

- **1 triangular coin is equal to 6 square coins**
- **1 square coin is equal to 4 circular coins**

Alice visits a market and buys some trinkets and a chalice costing 3 square coins and 1 circular coin. If she pays with a triangular coin, how much change will she have left over?

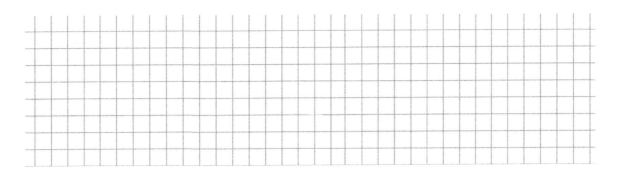

Answer:_____

10.

$$L, cm^2, km/h, m, km^2, km/s, ml,$$

Choose one unit from the list above to complete the sentences below:

a) **Liz drove her car at 60____ for one hour.**

b) **My horse lives in a field which is about 2_____**

c) **Yesterday I bought a 500____ bottle of milk from the supermarket.**

11. There are two temperature scales commonly used in weather forecasts, Fahrenheit (°F) and Celsius (°C). The formula to convert from °C to °F is given below:

F = (C x 1.8) + 32

Where C is the temperature in Celsius and F is the temperature in Fahrenheit. Find the temperature in Fahrenheit for the following values of C:

a) 30

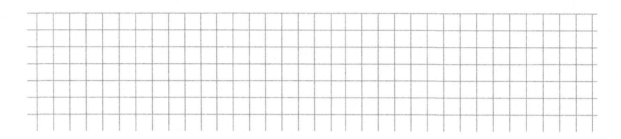

Answer:_____

b) 25

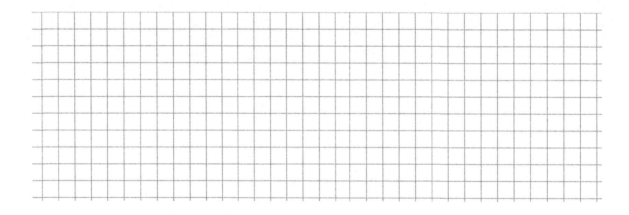

Answer:_____

c) -40

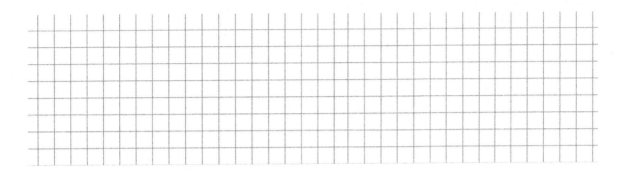

Answer:_____

12. Diego throws two dice and adds up their score. How many different ways are there for this total to be 9?

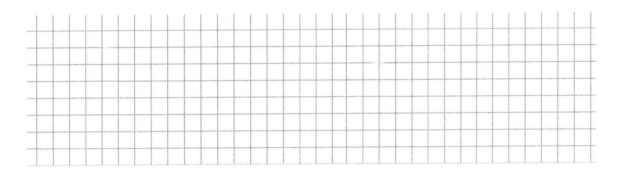

Answer:_____

13. Divide 4.2 by 0.2

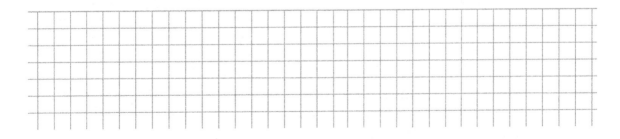

Answer:_____

14. In the number 436350, what is the difference in value between the two 3s?

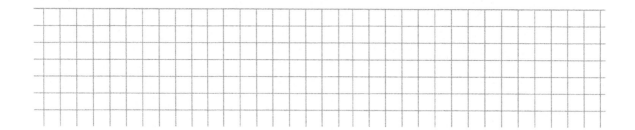

Answer:_____

15. Below we show two shapes, A and B.

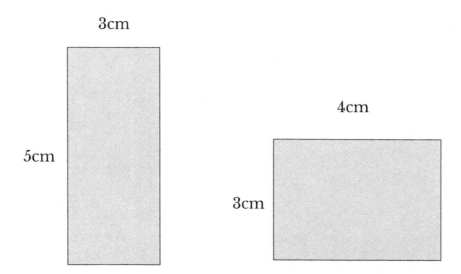

Find the area of the overlap when they are placed on top of one another as shown below:

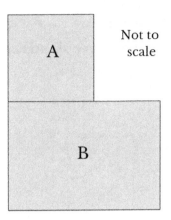

Not to scale

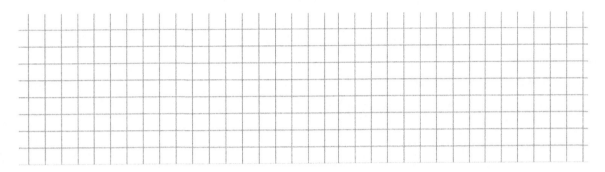

Answer:_____

16. If a square has area 36cm², what is its perimeter?

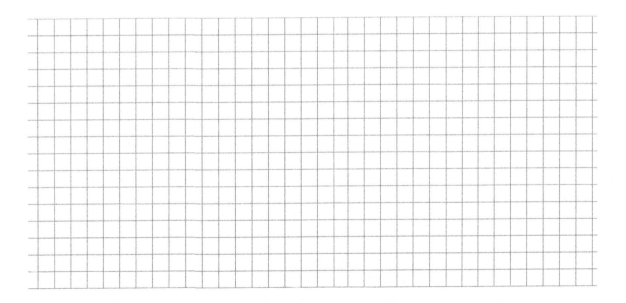

Answer:_____

17. a. Write down a sequence of 3 numbers, all less than 10, whose mean is smaller than their median.

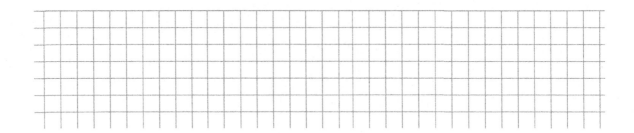

Answer:_____

b. Write down a sequence of 5 numbers, all less than 10, whose mode is bigger than the mean.

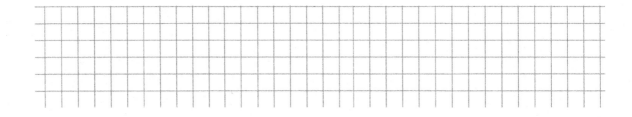

Answer:_____

18. Take a look at the following shape:

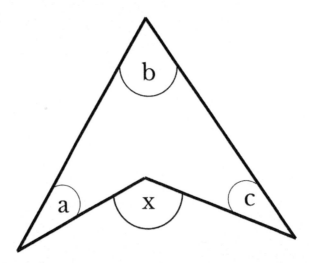

Given that:

- **a= 52**
- **b= 61**
- **c = 52**

Find x.

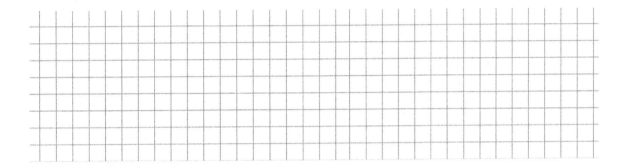

Answer:_____

19. Sisyphus pushes a boulder up a hill 500m every day. In the night, it rolls back down 250m. How many days and nights pass before the boulder reaches 5km up the hill? Leave your answer in the number of days and the number of nights.

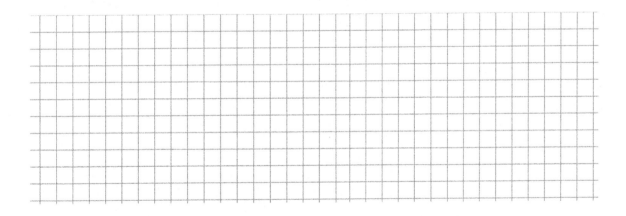

Answer:_____

20. The time is 12pm. On a clock face, as the minute hand sweeps in one full rotation, the hour hand sweeps continuously at a constant rate from 12 to 1. Thus at 12:30 the hour hand is halfway between 12 and 1.

a. What is the angle between the hour hand and minute hand at this time? (Calculate the angle from the hour hand to the minute hand in the clockwise direction).

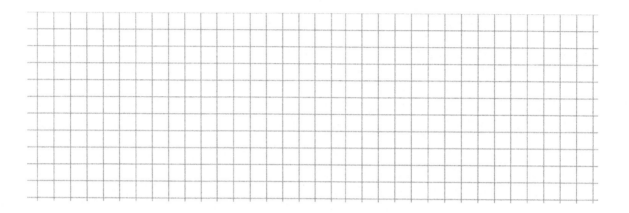

Answer:_____

b. What is the angle between the hour and the minute hand at 2:45? (Calculate the angle from the hour hand to the minute hand in the clockwise direction).

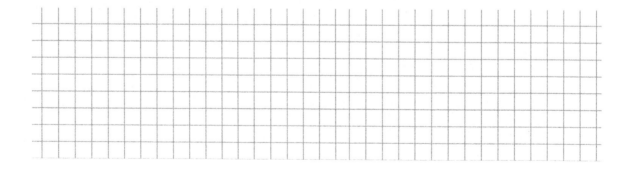

Answer:_____

Answers and Guidance

1. The distance from London to Edinburgh is 400 miles. 5 miles is approximately 8 kilometres.

Calculate the approximate distance from London to Edinburgh in kilometres.

If we know 5 miles are 8 kilometres then we just need to know how many lots of 5 miles are in 400 miles, and we can multiply this figure by 8 in order to find the distance in kilometres from London to Edinburgh. So we need to calculate 400 / 5 = 80. Then multiply 80 x 8 = 640. So the answer is 640km.

Answer: <u>640km</u>

2. Marcus thinks of a number (in Roman numerals)

He adds IX and multiplies by V.

His answer is LV.

What was his number? Write your answer in Roman numerals.

Marcus's answer is LV, which is 55 in Roman numerals. We know to get there, he multiplied by 5 after adding 9 to his starting number. So now we just need to work backwards. 55 / 5 = 11. Then subtracting 9 we have that Marcus's starting number was 2, which is II in Roman numerals.

Answer: II

3. How many odd numbers between 1000 and 1300 contain at least one 2 in their digits?

We can first notice that the first digit in any number between 1000 and 1300 will be 1, so we only have 3 other digits to worry about. The last digit can never be 2, as then the number will be even. So we only need to count how many times one of the second or third digit will be 2, **and** the number is odd. Either the number is of the form 102X, 112X or 12XY, where X and Y are any digits.

In the first and second cases, X = 1, 3, 5, 7, 9 are possible. This gives 10 numbers.

In the third case, all the numbers between 1200 and 1299 (inclusive) have a two in them, and half are odd. This gives 50 numbers to count between 1200 and 1300.

Thus the final answer is 50 + 10 = 60.

Answer: 60

4. In a gym there are 72 people. If 25% are running on a tread-mill, and ⅓ are lifting weights, how many are doing something else?

We need to work out 25% of 72 and ⅓ of 72.

In the first case, 25% of 72 is 72 / 4 = 36 / 2 = 18, while in the second case ⅓ of 72 is the same as 72 / 3 = 24.

Now we need to subtract both of these from 72, which is 72 - 18 - 24 = 30.

So the answer is 30.

Answer: 30

5. If a triangle has sides which are all whole numbers, and its perimeter is 11cm. How many different triangles with these properties are possible?

Be careful! Remember that the nature of a triangle is such that the length of no two sides can add up to less than the length of the third. For instance, a triangle with sides 1, 2, 4 does not exist, as 1+2=3 < 4.

We will start by listing all the possible triangles taking into account only the constraint of the sides summing 11; and once we have done that we will rule out the possibilities that do not satisfy the final condition about the smallest sides adding up to less than the longest one.

The three sides of the triangle must be positive whole numbers. So the minimum side length is 1cm. We will start here and work upwards until we run out of possible triangles. I will use the notation (1, 1, 9) to describe a triangle with side lengths 1cm, 1cm and 9cm. Then the triangles (1,1,9), (1,9,1) and (9,1,1) are all equivalent. We are looking for different triangles. We will write all our side lengths in increasing order, to ensure we don't count one triangle more than once.

After (1,1,9) we increase one of the side lengths by 1. This leaves (1,2,8). Now we have two choices: we can either increase the same side length or the other one. We could increase the third, but if we leave that one to be determined by the other two, we can be sure we won't count any triangles twice. Let's first cover all triangles which have at least one side length which is 1cm. Then we have (1,1,9), (1,2,8), (1,3,7), (1,4,6), (1,5,5). And now note if we increase our side length again, this gives (1,6,4), which we have already counted. So far we have found 5 possible triangles

Now we go back to (1,2,8) and increment the first side length, to get (2,2,7), and increase the second side length as much as we can again: (2,3,6), (2,4,5). Any higher and we repeat ourselves. This adds 3, to make a total of 8 possible triangles.

We increment the first length again to start at (3,3,5). Now we only have (3,4,4) as another possibility. This adds a further 2 to our total so we have 10 possible triangles

We can go no higher, as if we let the first side length be 4cm, then since we were writing in increasing order to avoid double counting, we would need to start with at least (4,4,4) which has a perimeter of 12cm, and is thus too big. So our answer is that there are 10 possible triangles.

One nice way to organize this question is to use a table. Once you realise that the third side length is determined by the other two, we can use a two by two table to record all the possibilities we have tried.

The columns record the length of the second side. The rows record the length of the first side.

Finally, it takes a lot longer to write out this solution than to follow this logic in your head and write out the answer. If you didn't get the solution, try to follow the sequence of steps which should get you there in a principled fashion.

	1	2	3	4	5
1	(1,1,9)	(1,2,8)	(1,3,7)	(1,4,6)	(1,5,5)
2	(2,2,7)	(2,3,6)	(2,4,5)		
3	(3,3,5)	(3,4,4)			

Now we must rule out the "impossible" triangles. Clearly, the first row must be eliminated almost entirely, as only the last one is a plausible triangle (1+1=2 < 9, 1+2=3 < 8, etc.). Of the second row, only the last one satisfies the condition, because 2+4=6 > 5. Both triangles in the last row exist as well.

The answer is therefore **four**: (1,5,5), (2,4,5), (3,3,5), (3,4,4).

Answer: 4

6. Which of the numbers below gives the best estimate of the amount of milk in a bowl of cereal:

1ml   10ml   100ml   1L   10L

1ml is around the amount of liquid in an eye drop pipette: you would hardly notice this much milk in your cereal. 10ml is around the capacity of a kitchen spoon, so again not sufficient for a bowl. 1L is a significant amount — around a quarter of the average amount of fluid you consume in a day. This would require a very large breakfast! The fact that 1L is too much also rules out 10L.

As such, we can assert with confidence that the correct answer is 100ml.

Answer: <u>100ml</u>

7. A box of gloves contains 4 pairs of gloves. What is the smallest number of gloves I need to take out of the box to guarantee that I have both a left-hand glove and a right hand glove?

If we only take one glove out, let's assume that it's left-handed. Then the next glove we take out could be left or right handed, so taking just one is not enough to guarantee we have a pair.

If I have already taken 7 gloves out, however, then I either have 4 left-handed gloves and 3 right-handed gloves, or 3 left-handed gloves and 4 right-handed gloves. In either of these cases, I definitely have 3 pairs of gloves, so 7 is definitely sufficient. Clearly we can do it with less. So we need to consider the case where I draw out 4 gloves which are all of the same type, say left-handed, then when I draw another glove it must be right-handed, and thus I definitely have a pair.

We see this with any sequence of draws. After 5 draws there will always be at least one pair of one left and one right handed gloves.

Answer: <u>5</u>

8. I take my dog on a walk. She walks at 4km/h. Tibbles the cat walks 75% as fast as my dog. How long does it take Tibbles to walk 8km? Leave your answer in hours and minutes.

We can first work out Tibbles' speed. We convert 75% into a fraction, which is $^{75}/_{100} = ^3/_4$. Then $^3/_4$ of 4 is 3, so Tibbles walks at 3km/h.

Then we can work out that she will cover 1km every 20 minutes. So in 8 x 20 =160 minutes she will cover 8km. This is 2 hours and 40 minutes.

Answer: 2 hours and 40 minutes

9. In the Land of Nee, there are 3 types of coin. In order of value – from most valuable to least valuable – they are the triangular coin, the square coin, and the circular coin. We know the following information:

- **1 triangular coin is equal to 6 square coins**
- **1 square coin is equal to 4 circular coins**

Alice visits a market and buys some trinkets and a chalice costing 3 square coins and 1 circular coin. If she pays with a triangular coin, how much change will she have left over?

If this were regular currency, we might have a price of £5.10 and pay with £10. Then to find the answer we could simply complete the subtraction £10.00 - £5.10 = £4.90. The idea here is the same, but since we have a difficult currency, we have to be more careful.

Rather than subtracting, we can count up — we ask ourselves, how many coins do we need to add to the amount Alice pays in order to make one triangle? Starting at 3 squares and 1 circle, we know she would need to have 3 more circular coins in order to have the equivalent of 4 square coins in total. Then with 2 more square coins she would have a full triangle.

So her change should be **2 square coins and 3 circular ones**.

Candidates will also score the marks if they say **1 square coin and 7 circular coins OR 11 circular coins**.

Answer: 2 square coins and 3 circular coins OR 1 square coin & 7 circular coins OR 11 circular coins.

10.

L, cm^2, km/h, m, km^2, km/s, ml,

Choose one unit from the list above to complete the sentences below:

a) Liz drove her car at 60___ for one hour.

b) My horse lives in a field which is about 2___

c) Yesterday I bought a 500___ bottle of milk from the supermarket.

(a)

The first sentence is about the speed of a car, so we need a unit of speed. There are two options, either km/h or km/s. 60km/s is about 60 x 60 = 3600km/minute, which is much faster than any car can travel; so the answer must be km/h.

Answer: <u>km/h</u>

(b)

The second sentence is about an area, so we need a unit of area, which is either km^2 or cm^2. A horse covers an area of much more than $2cm^2$, so it would not even fit in a field of this size; accordingly, the answer must be $2km^2$, which is also a sensible size for a field.

Answer: <u>km^2</u>

(c)

The final sentence is about an amount of liquid, so we need either litres (L) or millilitres (ml). 500L is a huge volume of liquid — far more than you could buy in a supermarket in a single bottle — thus the answer must be ml.

Answer: <u>ml</u>

11. There are two temperature scales commonly used in weather forecasts, Fahrenheit (°F) and Celsius (°C). The formula to convert from °C to °F is given below:

F = (C x 1.8) + 32

Where C is the temperature in Celsius and F is the temperature in Fahrenheit. Find the temperature in Fahrenheit for the following values of C:

a) 30

b) 25

c) -40

(a)

Starting with a), the only really tricky bit is to do the multiplication properly. There are several ways to do this. We can just do the multiplication 30 x 1.8 — or slightly easier may be to notice that $1.8 = \frac{9}{5}$ and then find $30 \times \frac{9}{5} = \frac{30}{5} \times 9 = 6 \times 9 = 54$. So the first answer is $(30 \times 1.8) + 32 = 54 + 32 = 86$.

Answer: <u>86</u>

(b)

Doing the same thing again with b) we find $25 \times \frac{9}{5} = \frac{25}{5} \times 9 = 5 \times 9 = 45$ and $45 + 32 = 77$. So the answer to b) is 77.

Answer: <u>77</u>

(c)

Finally, we have to deal with negative numbers but the process is the same. First we find that $-40 \times \frac{9}{5} = \frac{^-40}{5} \times 9 = -8 \times 9 = -72$. Then adding 32 we get $-72 + 32 = -40$. So the answer to c) is -40. It is interesting to note that -40 is the point at which both Fahrenheit and Celsius are equal.

Answer: <u>-40</u>

12. Diego throws two dice and adds up their score. How many different ways are there for this total to be 9?

We need to count the number of ways two scores (each less than or equal to 6) can add up to 9. The possible sums are 6+3 or 5+4; however, each of these we need to count twice. That is because, for example, in the first case, either the first dice can show 6 and the second 3, or the first can show 3 and the second 6. We summarise this in the table below:

	Die 1	Die 2
Die 1	(3,6)	(5,5)
Die 2	(6,3)	(4,5)

Thus the answer is 4.

Answer: <u>4</u>

13. Divide 4.2 by 0.2.

There are several ways to do this. My preference would be to convert both numbers into fractions, then change the multiplication to division. We can write 0.2 as $\frac{1}{5}$ and 4.2 as $\frac{42}{10} = \frac{21}{5}$. Then $\frac{21}{5} \div \frac{1}{5} = \frac{21}{5} \times \frac{5}{1} = 21$.

Alternatively, we could note that 0.2 goes into 1 five times. As a result, to figure out how many times 0.2 goes into 4, we simply multiply 5 by 4, which gives us 20. Then we add one more 0.2 to give us 4.2. So 0.2 goes into 4.2 a total of 21 times!

Answer: <u>21</u>

14. In the number 436350, what is the difference in value between the two 3s?

The first 3 (reading left to right) represents 30,000 while the second 3 represents 300. Thus we just need to do the subtraction 30,000-300=29,700. So the answer is 29,700.

Answer: 29,700

15. Below we show two shapes, A and B.

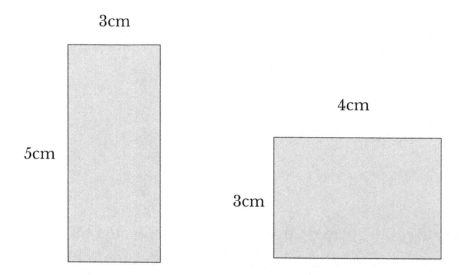

Find the area of the overlap when they are placed on top of one another as shown below:

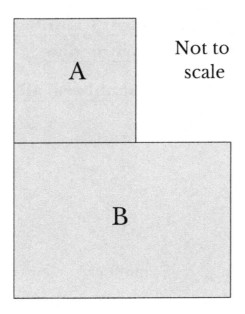

First we find the lengths of the overlapping region, then we just multiply these together. Using the information we have about A and B, we can see that the overlapping region has height 3cm and width 3cm. Thus it has area **9cm²**.

Answer: 9cm²

16. If a square has area 36cm², what is its perimeter?

A square has the same lengths to all its sides: let's call its side length X. Then the area is $X^2=36cm^2$. If we recognise that 36 is a square number, we can see that its side-length is 6. So the perimeter is 4 x 6 = **24cm**.

Answer: 24cm

17. a. Write down a sequence of 3 numbers, all less than 10, whose mean is smaller than their median.

b. Write down a sequence of 5 numbers, all less than 10, whose mode is bigger than the mean.

(a)

First we need a sequence of 3 numbers where the middle number is smaller than the mean. Let's pick a random middle point like 7. We need to pick two more numbers.

The smaller number must be closer to 7 than the larger number. So choosing 6 and 9 will do. You could find this by trial and error, or by noticing that the larger the biggest number is, the more it increases the mean.

If a candidate gives any three numbers under 10, and the middle number they've chosen is closer to the smallest number than it is to the largest number, they will score the marks.

(b)

For the second part, we just need the most common number to be bigger than the mean. But they should also be close to the mean to keep the mean low. So something like:

1,2,7,8,8.

The mean is never going to be as big as the biggest number, as it will be dragged down by the others.

There are multiple correct answers. **If you add up all the numbers the candidate has given and divide the result by 5, and that**

figure is smaller than the number that appears most frequently in their sequence, then it is a correct answer.

18. Take a look at the following shape:

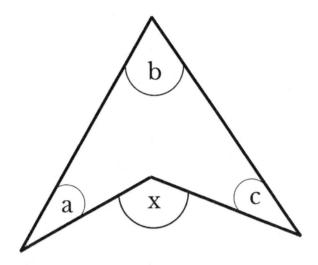

Given that:

- **a= 52**
- **b= 61**
- **c = 52**

Find x.

We know angles in a quadrilateral add up to 360, so the final angle not labelled in the shape must be 360 - 52 -61 - 52 = 195. We also know that angles around a point add up to 360. So x = 360 - 195 = 165.

Answer: 165

19. Sisyphus pushes a boulder up a hill 500m every day. In the night, it rolls back down 250m. How many days and nights pass before the boulder reaches 5km up the hill? Leave your answer in the number of days and the number of nights.

We could keep adding days and nights until we hit 5000m (5km).

For example 500 - 250 + 500 - 250…. Or we could notice that over the course of one day and one night, the net movement of the boulder is 250m. Thus every day and night that passes, the boulder moves 250m. Then over say 4 days and nights, the boulder moves 1000m. So logically after 20 days it will reach 5000m. We have to be careful however! On the 19th day the boulder will begin at 4500m up the hill, Sisyphus will push the boulder up to 5000m, then it will roll back down to 475m in the night. On the 20th day Sisyphus will push the boulder up the hill to 5250m and roll back down in the night to 5000m. So in reality the first time the boulder will reach 500m will be after 19 days and 18 nights.

Answer: <u>19 days and 18 nights</u>

20. The time is 12pm. On a clock face, as the minute hand sweeps in one full rotation, the hour hand sweeps continuously at a constant rate from 12 to 1. Thus at 12:30 the hour hand is halfway between 12 and 1.

a. What is the angle between the hour hand and minute hand at this time? (Calculate the angle from the hour hand to the minute hand in the clockwise direction).

b. What is the angle between the hour and the minute hand at 2:45? (Calculate the angle from the hour hand to the minute hand in the clockwise direction).

(a)

It would be wrong to answer 180°. This is the angle formed when the hour hand is pointing directly upwards and the minute hand directly downwards. However, we were just explicitly told that the hour hand will be halfway between 12 and 1, so the angle the hour and minute hand will make is less than 180. The angle between each hour is $360/12 = 30°$. So half of this is 15. Thus the angle these two hands make is 180 - 15 = 165°.

Answer: 165°

(b)

To get the second part, we will first work out the angle between the minute hand at 45mins past the hour, and the hour hand at 2pm, then we will subtract from this angle the hour hand sweeps between 2 and 3pm. We can notice that when the minute hand is at 45min it is pointing to the number 9, thus there are 7 subdivisions of 30° between 2 and 9 or an angle of 7 x 30 = 210°. Now at 2:45 the hour hand has covered ¾ of the distance between the hour 2 and the hour 3, so we need to subtract from 210° an angle of size ¾ x 30 = 3 x $30/4$= 3 x 7.5 = 22.5. This gives us the answer, which is:

210 - 22.5 = **187.5**.

Answer: 187.5°

Printed in Great Britain
by Amazon

47686964R00159